Where Have All the Young Ones GONE?
Connecting and Reconnecting Young Adults to God and the church

Where Have All the Young Ones GONE?

Connecting and Reconnecting Young Adults to God and the church

Nina M. Thompson, DMin,

Foreword by Peter J. Bellini, Ph.D.

roseofsharonnow@gmail.com
nicheprandcomm@sbcglobal.net

Where Have All the Young Ones GONE?
Connecting and Reconnecting Young Adults to God and the church
© 2017 by Nina M. Thompson,
roseofsharonnow@gmail.com
Rose of Sharon Ministries, Inc.

Cover Art: NICHE Public Relations and Communications

ALL RIGHTS RESERVED. This book contains material protected under International and Federal Copyright Laws and Treaties. Any unauthorized reprint or use of this material is prohibited. No part of this book may be reproduced or transmitted in any form or by any means, electronic or mechanical, including photocopying, recording, or by any information storage and retrieval system without express written permission from the author.

For permission requests, email the publisher with the subject line "copyright permission" at:

Rose of Sharon Ministries
Nina M. Thompson, DMin
roseofsharonnow@gmail.com
or: nicheprandcomm@sbcglobal.net

Unless otherwise indicated, all scripture quotations are taken from the King James Version of the Holy Bible.

Published by: Nina Thompson, NICHE Public Relations and Communications
ISBN: 978-0-991-0287-2-6

Printed in the United States

CONTENTS

Foreword vi
Preface ix
Acknowledgements xiii
Introduction – Why Have all the Young Ones Gone? 15

FOUNDATIONS

Chapter 1 – Research Overview 22
    A. Research Context
    B. Ministry Model
    C. Problem Statement
    D. Research Methodology
    E. Major Assumptions and Objectives

Chapter 2 – Research Foundations 32
    A. Biblical – A Glimpse at Jeremiah and Timothy
    B. Historical – Led to Purpose Fulfillment
    C. Theological - God, the Father, Son and Holy Spirit
    D. Theoretical – Developmental Theories in Emerging Adults

Chapter 3 – Methodology 97
    A. Gift Identification and Activation
    B. Mentoring - Equipping, Engaging, Empowering
    C. Leadership Development and Peer-to-Peer Mentoring

Chapter 4 – Project Analysis and Methodology, Summary, Conclusions 107

APPENDIX
    A. Survey Tools ....
    B. Participant Testimonies/Essays ....
    C. Spiritual Gifts Assessment ....
    D. Benchmarks for College Age Ministries, United Methodist Church

BIBLIOGRAPHY ....

FOREWORD

Dr. Peter Bellini, Ph.D.

We are in the midst of a global quake that is erupting from multiple seismic shifts of the cultural and ideological plates that undergird our age, and out of the dust and ashes of our former realties, we are feeling the tremors of a "Great Emergence" as Phyllis Tickle put it in her groundbreaking book of the same title. Some have simplified this complex metamorphosis as an emergence of an age of "posts", postmodern, post-postmodern, postcolonial, post western, post-national, post-industrial, post-truth, post-fact, post-trend, post gender, post-racial etc, and post Christian, and even post-post Christian. These "posts" are signposts that indicate the multitude of seismic shifts taking place in our day. Each of these and more have greatly impacted Christianity, including its decline, spread, methods, perceptions, interaction, and responses to a world that is watching Christianity explode in the Global South and East and eroding into oblivion in the West. How will the church work through the maze of these *post* transitions and reach people with the good news in a new way? Where does this leave this generation and the next that identify as spiritual but not institutionally religious?

Nina Thompson cites that in "2000, nearly one-quarter of people ages 18-29 described their religion as none, and since 2005, the unchurched segment among this age group increased from 44% to 52%." Thompson's work comes straight out of the cracks and margins of such seismic shifts amidst the fiery racial tension and violence in Ferguson, Missouri, home of Michael Brown who was fatally shot by a white police officer. Her response is not the typical church response to throw more programs or dollars at the problem or to hide within the four stain-glassed walls of the church. Her response is the Holy Spirit. People, young people, need to get connected and reconnected to God, and there is only one way and that is through God's self, the Holy Spirit.

This book comes out of Nina Thompson's doctoral research as a student at United Theological Seminary where I served as her doctoral mentor for the project. Her work "seeks to demonstrate that activating spiritual gifts in young adults, complemented by mentoring and training, will increase their commitment to God and church," as she concisely puts it in her project abstract. The Holy Spirit through the workings of the *charismata,* or spiritual gifts, can transcend the borders and boundaries of this post-world in which we live and navigate the unexplored terrain, where church programs and personalities have failed to travel, and can speak fresh divine revelation to the broken condition of the world that will minister healing, resurrection and shalom. Teaching young people to hear the voice of God under the direction of a mentor-based contextualized program, I believe is the beginning of a revelation-based revolution that will enable the church to once again be at the forefront of the inbreaking of the Kingdom of light through the kingdom of darkness.

Dr. P. Bellini is an ordained Elder in the West Ohio Conference of The United Methodist Church and has served in urban ministry for more than 25 years. He has been a leader in every facet of ministry, including new church starts, church turnarounds, mergers, local church renewal, discipleship and leadership training, inner city and global missions and several marketplace ministries. He has also served and taught on several continents, including Europe, Africa and Asia and currently serves as the Associate Professor of Evangelization in the Heisel Chair and the Director of Non-Degree Programs with United Theological Seminary in Dayton, Ohio. He teaches in the areas of Church Renewal, Global Charismatic Studies, Missiology, Evangelism, Intercultural and Interreligious Encounter, and Urban Studies. His interest is in the intersection of pneumatology and holiness, including themes such as Trinitarian mission theology and theosis and the theology, history and practices of renewal movements (Methodism, the Holiness movement, the Pentecostal-Charismatic movement, and the Global Renewalist movement of today).

<u>Publications</u>

Truth Therapy: Renewing Your Mind with the Word of God, Xulon, 2010.

Participation: Epistemology and Mission Theology, Emeth, 2011.

Truth Therapy: Expanded Edition. Wipf and Stock, 2015.

"Mental Health and the Christian Life," in *A Noble Mind: Expanding Worldview through Social Issues*, edited by Terry Swan and Curtis Lee Jr., Guardian Books, 2016.

PREFACE

Getting to God is no easy journey.

I was only able to begin to walk the path that would expose me to the true Spirit of God after much pain, patience and positioning. Prior to developing a true connection to the Holy Spirit, I had stopped attending church consistently for more than 25 years. During those years, which began in my early 20s, I had also developed a level of dislike for "church people" and church leadership, and began to operate under the premise that while I believed in God, I had to depend on myself and my own strength to accomplish things. My frustration with my spiritual journey had led me to a place where my Spirit was not getting its daily feeding, and all I believed that I had was a book of scripture that I had a difficult time remembering; but indeed, God had planted a seed of yearning in me that could not be satisfied until the two of us were in full and complete relationship. God had purpose for my life; even if I didn't know it at the time.

I thought that I was making my own decisions and charting my own course, but God's hand was indeed leading me through experience after experience; experiences which ultimately would lead me to my purpose and to stronger relationship with God.

Where Have All the Young Ones GONE? Connecting and Reconnecting Young Adults to God and the church was being written throughout this entire journey. Ultimately, however, the book came to publication as a result of my attendance at United Theological Seminary in Dayton, where the requirement of a doctoral thesis led me through a path of personal reflection and examination. This journey created a fresh, new desire within me to provide strategies to people, especially emerging adults that would lead to true spiritual relationship with God beyond remembering scriptures, attending church and asking for help. My goal was to take what I had learned while traveling on my journey to God, compliment my personal discoveries with instruction received from pastors and spiritual guides, and formalize both of those pieces with the research-based thesis that I eventually produced. My ultimate plan was to help young adults successfully navigate a spirit-to-Spirit lived relationship with God during what is the most critical and most receptive time of their lives.

The good news is that God had placed me under the tutelage of "mentors" who clearly understood the difficulties of this journey and were anointed enough to make it plain and clear. The other good news is that my research, while challenging and tedious for me, not only proved what the leaders had taught me, but also brought forth a wealth of wisdom and knowledge given to me by God through the Holy Spirit, which was validated by my own life's journey.

This book is my contribution to the journey to adulthood; one fraught with desires to understand ourselves and others better, and to gain more clarity around ourselves as part of a larger group. It is a time of heightened insecurity, potentially fluid relationships, and growing pains. It is a time when we yearn for greater understanding and often find that difficult to achieve with life's limitations.

But, it also is a time of opportunity, a time when we are more open to leadership and guidance that helps us to better examine and understand our purpose. It can be a time when, if we are properly introduced to the life-changing relationship with God through the Holy Spirit (Holy Trinity), and properly directed on how to establish and maintain that relationship, we can walk in a greater understanding of true purpose, true positioning and true peace.

As primarily a young adult minister for the past 6 years (not including the 12 or more years during which I found myself "ministering" to young adults not aware of what I was doing), and a college English and Oral Communications instructor, I have consistently applied these strategies in responding to young adults who seek me out for support, prayer and guidance. I have learned, especially within the past several years that the outcomes greatly substantiate the research time after time; whether the tools are applied in a stable and consistent environment, or by consistent telephone ministry to emerging adults in need of spiritual guidance and assistance. Each and every time they end up establishing a greater understanding of who God created them to be and the spiritual gifts that they have been given in order to become those people, a thirst for greater wisdom and knowledge of God, and a partnership with a ministry group or church in order to put what they have learned into practice. They end up with a desire to serve

God in Spirit and in Truth; a spiritual place where we all hope to eventually meet with God over and over again.

Acknowledgments

Thank you God for showing me who I am, and letting me in on the plans that you have for me. I am so excited about tomorrow, and the next day, and the next day.

Thanks to my mother, Catherine, and all of my siblings Linda, Ki, Peggy and Malcolm, and a host of nieces and nephews and close friends, for putting up with me during the tough growing seasons; seasons when I was not always so excited about tomorrow. Your whispered and shouted prayers are working wonders.

Thanks Dr. Peter Bellini for walking me through the completion of this research project, and showing me that it was not only okay to believe all that I believed, but that my beliefs were completely necessary to the completion of God's work within me. I pray that this work honors the effort and the recognitions that you awarded me during graduation services. I love you, beautiful Maria, Paola, and even the son that I haven't had a chance to meet. You guys truly have a soft space in my heart and I cherish your friendship.

Thanks Zita for your meticulous read of this book. You not only served as my editor, but you are and have always been a dear friend. I cannot thank you enough for not only editing, but actually trying to make me feel better for the hard work that you had to do by bragging about how you enjoyed the read and how much you learned. You know me and you know I greatly appreciated that. Love you lots.

Thank you to Pastors Pamela and John Dillon of Agape Time Ministries, Inc. Through your ministry work, I had my first glimpse of what it looked like to truly be in relationship with God through His Holy Spirit and confirmation of my call to young adult ministry. Your tireless dedication to me and the other members of Agape Time Ministries, Inc., and your desire to prepare me to work in all of my areas of gifting, have not fallen on fallow ground.

Finally, thanks to Rev. F. Willis Johnson, Jr., pastor of Wellspring UMC in Ferguson. You not only suggested seminary, but you also talked me through some very rough times during the first few semesters. While I knew that I could not quit, you reminded me that my assignment was more important than my feelings.

Introduction

Why Have All the Young Ones Gone?

Young adults are leaving churches in droves. No matter what charismatic spin is put on this, the numbers of emerging adults seen in church pews, those between the ages of eighteen and thirty, are steadily dwindling. Within this age group there also are of course, fewer new church memberships.

This failure of the church to attract emerging adults threatens its very existence. A recipe of fewer young people attending and older people aging out ultimately means church closures due to a decrease in memberships, professions of faith, and attendance. This trend could also influence the number of people who help to support and sustain the church's longtime mandate and mission: to preach the gospel, make disciples and to serve and support the less fortunate among us.

This exodus is not recent news. [1]As early as 1999, there was an indicated drop in the number of both millenials and emerging adults who attended church at least once per year from 58% to 56%. In addition, this same study indicated that the percentage of those who do not affiliate directly with any particular religion rose from 16% in 2007, to 23% in 2014, and this is particularly pronounced

---

[1] Pew Forum on Religious and Public Life, Religious Landscape Study June 4 – September 30, 2014, Pew Research Group, http://www.pewforum.org/religious-landscape-study/

among young adults. [2] In 2016, only 37,953 adults were baptized, where just 11 years earlier, that number was 76,605, according to the Center for Applied Research in the Apostolate conducted by Georgetown University. [3]

Author Dennis McCallum in *Members of One Another: How to Build a Biblical Ethos into Your Church* says that while many churches have opted to offer seemingly more progressive options for church participation such as texting or blogging about the content of services, or upgrading music ministries in an attempt to be more contemporary, these attempts are wrong sighted and do not focus on the primary outcome of raising individuals who commit to long-term service to God. "Most churches have little or nothing going on with college students – the most promising age range for raising up workers who serve God long-term. I think it goes to show that churches are more interested in adults who pay the bills than in raising up workers."[4]

When examining what ideally attracts these individuals, research has reflected repeatedly that one of the major needs expressed by those in this age category is to have an "experience" during the worship service. Emerging adults have said that they want a connection with God, Jesus and the Holy Spirit; one

---

[2] Pew Forum on Religious and Public Life, Religious Landscape Study June 4 – September 30, 2014, Pew Research Group, http://www.pewforum.org/religious-landscape-study/

[3] Center for Applied Research in the Apostolate, 2016, http://cara.georgetown.edu/frequently-requested-church-statistics/

[4] Dennis McCallum, *Members of One Another: How to Build a Biblical Ethos into Your Church* (Houston, TX: New Paradigm Publishing, 2010), 297.

that moves beyond mere ritual and the sacraments. Has the church, in trying to recreate and establish additional "bells and whistles" to attract people, neglected the very central elements that connect the everyday Christian life with God?

Jason E. Vickers, in *Invocation and Assent: The Making and Remaking of Trinitarian Theology,* states that "the Trinity has been marginalized and the connection between the Trinity and Christian life, has been substantially diminished."[5] Vickers notes that while the Trinity was indispensable for Christian ecclesial materials and practices, it has been overused and its power diminished within the church. Many Christians are aware of the Holy Trinity and can state that it includes the Father, the Son and the Holy Spirit. Few, however, can offer an explanation of the Trinity or how it functions within the life of a believer.

Lester Agyei McCorn adds that the Holy Spirit is inexplicably tied to the resurrection of people. "It becomes clear, that the restoration of the nation and the resurrection of the people are contingent upon the connection of holy people with the Holy Spirit."[6] In *Standing on Holy Common Ground: An Afrocentric Ministry Approach to Prophetic Community Engagement.* McCorn states that, "The key to transforming our dry bones is a life-transforming experience with the power of the

---

[5] Jason E. Vickers, *Invocation and Assent: The Making and Remaking of Trinitarian Theology* (Grand Rapids, MI: W. Eerdman's Publishing Company, 2008), 25.

[6] Lester McCorn, *Standing on Holy Common Ground: An Afrocentric Ministry Approach to Prophetic Community Engagement* (Chicago, IL: MMGI Books, 2013), 84.

Holy Spirit. We must call on the Spirit to motivate these bones to action."[7]

According to McCorn, the transformative power of God in individual lives lies in that being's ability and opportunity to connect to the renewing and transforming power of the Holy Spirit.

As early as 1995, experts in this area put out the call for increased and focused Holy Spirit engagement. In *SOUL FEAST: An Invitation to the Christian Spiritual Life,* Marjorie J. Thompson suggests that the time may be right for a more spiritual and Holy Spirit-focused approach that young adults seem to be calling for. "Both within and beyond traditional faith communities, a hunger for spiritual depth and integrity is gaining momentum."[8] "We have come to believe that only a power beyond life can give meaning to our choices and circumstances. For some of us, our hunger is spiritual."[9]

If these experts, whose input ranges from the late 1990's to present day, are to be believed as research indicates that they are, there seem to be very practical steps that can be taken in order to increase the commitment to church and God among this age group. In addition, experts in the field of human development believe individuals within this age group are strongly focused on

---

[7] Ibid., 87.

[8] Marjorie. J. Thompson, *SOUL FEAST: An Invitation to the Christian Spiritual Life* (Louisville, KY: Westminster John Knox Press, 1995), 1.

[9] Ibid.

exploring attitudes, values and life possibilities. This is a perfect time to introduce new concepts that relate to identity and purpose, while attitudes and values are being broadened and readjusted. Additionally, this time of life provides an opportunity to introduce concepts related to church, if this information is undergirded by mentoring that helps these young adults determine who they are, what they were created to do, and how church and God fit into that model.

  Moving forward with these ideas in mind, this project focuses on applying solutions that create real and lasting spiritual connections to God through the indwelling of the Holy Spirit. That is the primary part of the recipes that will be used in the model. These connections must show emerging adults how they are connected to God, both individually and collectively, and how that connection informs and helps them to navigate their lives. In addition, any connections applied must also guide emerging adults through this process with the support of committed, spiritually astute, mentors; mentors who focus on understanding and addressing their real everyday needs and concerns with few or no boundaries, and who are consistently present and available to answer tough questions and provide insight. At the same time, these mentors must allow them both opportunity and space to expand and grow, to ask questions and yet formulate their own answers, and to test new ideas and theories that may not immediately appear to line up with the church or the Bible.

Finally, emerging adults must be given the opportunity to develop the tools that will lead them to success, not only as members of a church or followers of Christ, but also in everyday life. This opportunity could come through guided and participative teaching that focuses on learning both leadership and biblical principles and developing a spiritual basis for decision-making. It must explore mainstream values, offer help navigating relationships and personal choices, and provide examples of the practical application of godly principles to everyday life choices, among other things.

The proposed model of ministry will increase commitment to God and the church in emerging adults by guiding them to identify and practice using their Holy Spirit given gifts, while being supported with mentoring and undergirded by leadership training. It is based on a belief that if prophetic church leadership focused on helping young adults discover and develop their Holy Spirit given gifts, while arming them with biblical principles and mentoring that helps them apply these Christian principles to their everyday lives, the impetus might then exists that results in increased church membership and overall commitment to God.

To explore this model, chapter one outlines the ministry model and context, the problem statement, research methodologies and major assumptions and objectives. Chapter 2 examines the basis and foundation of the research including biblical support, historical support, theological support and theoretical support where development theories are outlined. Chapter 3 examines the methodology for the study while chapter 4 provides an analysis, summary and conclusions.

Chapter 1

Research Overview

According to a 2007 Lifeway Research Study and a more recent 2010 study conducted by the Pew Research Group, multitudes of people of all races and cultures are dropping out of the church. While African Americans did indeed tend to experience a lesser drop in church attendance and participation over the years than Caucasian or Hispanic adults, declines have been noted among all races since 1991.[10] In its recent study of religion and public life, the Pew Research Group found that not only was there a decrease in attendance, but there also were decreases in frequency of prayer, especially among those categorized as "religiously unaffiliated" and those aged 18-30.[11] Many churches are at a loss for what to do.

The highest levels of loss in church attendance seem to be occurring among emerging adults and college age individuals. These individuals can be critical to the long-term stability of the church, so this loss can prove very detrimental to the church. Some churches have attempted to shift gears by offering more progressive options for church participation such as allowing

---

[10] George Barna, "Major Faith Shifts Evident Among Whites, Blacks and Hispanics Since 1991," *State of the Church Series 2011 Report*, (August 2, 2011), accessed November 24, 2013, https://www.barna.org/barna-update/faith-spirituality/510-major-faith-shifts-evident-among-whites-blacks-and-hispanics-since-1991#.UpfzvnchRDE.

[11] Pew Forum on Religious and Public Life, Religious Landscape Study June 4 – September 30, 2014, Pew Research Group, http://www.pewforum.org/religious-landscape-study/

texting during church service, blogging to others about the content of a sermon as it is being delivered, or encouraging electronic friends like those on Facebook, to listen while the sermon is being streamed electronically. Others have upgraded their music ministries, offering a more contemporary repertoire. Seemingly, those attempts have failed. While church leaders do indeed seem to be conquering some of these electronic marketing tools, there still has been no substantial increase in interest or attendance within this age group.

Church leaders seem dumbfounded. Should they focus on reaching, converting and retaining future generations, or maintaining and sustaining those already committed to their church? Is there a simple but focused strategy that would help church leadership to maintain the support of older, long-term church members, while solidifying the memberships of young, emerging adults and college-age individuals? More importantly, can churches serve the spiritual needs of older members and younger members at the same time? Finally, does any of this matter if churches become obsolete due to a failure to grow?

The picture doesn't look too great, but what if the solution simply lay in the obvious: connecting or reconnecting these young adults to God and the church by helping them to identify their God-given gifts and talents; the knowledge of which could eventually propel them to fulfill their ordained, spiritual purposes? This could lead them not only back to God but also back to the church where guidance, mentoring and teaching could be strengthened. This project could potentially help to turn the tables on this trend by presenting new ways to attract young adults and thus leading them to choose long-term and lasting relationships with both God and the church.

A. <u>Research Context</u>

The research was conducted in Ferguson, Missouri "from August 2012 through August 2014," within the context of a church that the researcher was helping to launch. While this ministry model could potentially have been applied in any church, the church launch provided an opportunity to create a research group that would include participants who were emerging adults, were not regular church attendees, who had limited knowledge of God and God's operation in the lives of believers, and who expressed a desire to understand their relationship to God, the church, and the world around them.

The context also was the right testing ground because it provided an environment open to innovation in that it was both a United Methodist church encompassing the Wesleyan ideas concerning the existence of spiritual gifts, and a new church launch. The platform of United Methodism is open to the research approach and the newness of the church meant creative ideas and approaches could be accommodated.

The context location in a smaller suburb outside of the larger City of St. Louis, undergirded by its status as a new church plant, also was beneficial to conducting this type of research. It is important that participants who are asked to become engaged in understanding concepts and performing activities that are completely new to them be allowed to do these things in a comfortable, yet new environment. The research context pulled them away from the inner city, where many of them grew up and became familiar with specific social, cultural and spiritual mores, and offered them the opportunity to examine additional social and spiritual contextual ideas, within a new environment that they would ultimately help to construct. The fact that they could build their own reality as related to church participation and relationship with God, proved instrumental in their continued participation in the research project.

B. Ministry Model

The focus was on emerging adults because research indicates that this is where the steepest decline in church attendance and belief in God is actually occurring. In addition, these years of life, between the ages of 18 and 30, offer the greatest opportunities for individuals to form new and lasting connections.

This project to examine spiritual gifts and increase relationships with God in young adults had its birthing in this context, but it is definitely the result of the researcher's experiences both within the church as an emerging adult, and with young adults as an older individual. As a young adult, while bouncing from church to church, I finally decided that the church could not give me the type and depth of relationship that I wanted with God. So I became an infrequent, uncommitted church attendee. This challenged surfaced again later in life as I began to inadvertently serve as a "young adult minister" to college-aged adults, after they seemed to perpetually and consistently be drawn to me. What I noted was that same desire; a desire for a relationship with God that would provide clear direction on purpose and daily guidance.

Additionally, it was during this time that I was led to attend church again full-time, but not merely as a member, but as a lead member of the church plant team. I served as pastoral support, church administrator, young adult minister, facilities manager, finance person, grant writer, and a host of other things. I became fully ingrained in the church, so the theme of church reunification within the research, was both timely and appropriate.

Finally, a year after the church was launched I became a seminarian pursuing a doctor of ministry degree from United Theological Seminary in Dayton, Ohio. I noticed that my current ministry context would provide the perfect environment for developing a model of ministry that would allow me to explore the relationship between understanding God-given gifts and talents, leadership development and mentoring, as a systemic methodology to reconnect young adults to church and God.

Helping people discover their God-given gifts, talents and abilities, and teaching them how to grow in their understanding of God so that they can use these gifts, talents and abilities to God's glory has always been placed upon me as one of my God-ordained assignments. It is indeed now the focus of my current ministerial work through Rose of Sharon Ministries, Inc. and Yes to God young adult ministry.

C. Problem Statement

Obviously it is imperative that churches find a way to reach and retain younger church members and to attract potential and unaffiliated church goers, if they are to continue to grow, even to exist. Statistics indicate that this very important group of individuals, those under 30, are consistently missing from church pews and are moving toward a form of worship that pulls them away from traditional church attendance and participation. While some may still be seeking God and Godly relationship, that journey does not necessarily occur through the church.

According to the article, "Mainline Churches: The Real Reason for the Decline," as early as the late 1970s, a decline in attendance by many adolescents within the United Methodist Church was noted when those who had previously been confirmed, begin to drop out of church and not return. The article states that these were children of the members themselves who were leading the exodus while in the meantime; the average age of the membership was steadily increasing.[12] "One can sit today in the balcony of a typical United Methodist church and look over a congregation of graying and balding heads. Unless there is

---

[12] Benton Johnson, Dean R. Hoge and Donald A. Luidens, "Mainline Churches: The Real Reason for Decline," *First Things Magazine*, March 1993, accessed November 24, 2013, http://www.firstthings.com/article/1993/03/001-mainline-churches-the-real-reason-for-decline.

a surge of new recruits, rising death rates will diminish the ranks of the mainline denominations even further in the years ahead"[13] This trend, however, does not only affect the United Methodist church, but impacts all Christian affiliations across the United States.

While many churches have tried to change the way worship occurs or to alter other facets of the church services in order to accommodate a culture in the hopes of holding onto numbers, that simply does not work, according to Leroy Huizenga, Chair of the Department of Theology and Director of the Christian Leadership Center at the University of Mary in Bismarck, N.D. Christians must confess that it is not about numbers, but about fidelity, and letting the numbers fall where they may.[14] However, if these trends continue and a consistent decline in the numbers of young adults who are present and supportive of church remains, churches across the world may well see their numbers plummet into oblivion in years ahead.

Jason E. Vickers, in *Invocation and Assent: The Making and Remaking of Trinitarian Theology,* states that "the Trinity has been marginalized and the connection between the Trinity and Christian life, has been substantially diminished, and while the Trinity was indispensable for Christian ecclesial

---

[13] Ibid.

[14] Leroy Huizenga, "How Do Churches Grow," *First Things Magazine*, July 12, 2012, accessed October 2012, http://www.firstthings.com/onthesquare/2012/07/how-do-churches-grow.

materials and practices, it has been overused and its power diminished within the church."[15]

If this is true, and research suggests that it is, it is imperative that a ministry model be developed that stands true to the current principles outlined in biblical text, but that also embraces desires to have individual, productive and mission-focused relationships with God. Unless people understand what God has placed within them, they cannot hope to become what God has called them to be nor live out the purpose that is ordained for them. Continual frustration with the entire process will always be the end result and individuals will tend to develop and maintain their own strategies for seeking God or fail to continue seeking him, just as the researcher did. In line with that, the researcher suggests the following process for supporting such a ministry model.

D. Research Process and Methodology

The following process guided participants through Holy Spirit gift identification and use, and included additional components like leadership training and development and mentoring. Gift Identification and Activation provided opportunities to identify, understand and practice Holy Spirit gifts as outlined in First Corinthians and Ephesians, in a safe, non-threatening environment. Mentoring proved essential and took the form of spiritual support

---

[15] Jason E. Vickers, *Invocation and Assent: The Making and Remaking of Trinitarian Theology* (Grand Rapids, MI: W. Eerdman's Publishing Company, 2008), 195.

through prayer, life advisement, biblical teaching and discussions, individual meetings, and more. Mentoring also afforded an opportunity for each participant to meet with me to discuss personal issues and challenges. Further, leadership development was a process that included teaching of leadership principles based on John Maxwell's leadership principles, Agape Time Ministries, Inc. practices, and biblical leadership principles and examples. Also leadership development provided opportunities for participants to minister to and pray with others, teach, initiate ministries, plan activities, participate in church activities, and participate in small group meetings and ministry events.

E. **Major Assumptions and Objectives**

When launching into the study there are multiple assumptions that have been made related to the research topic. For example, emerging adults (young adults) are not attending church, or are leaving churches for multiple reasons. Therefore, one could conclude that unless something is done to turn around the decline in numbers, the very life of the historic church is at stake because young people help to maintain the ongoing generational participation in churches. Therefore, churches must become relevant to emerging adults, and must find solutions to offer greater spiritual experiences, which is what emerging adults are searching for. Additionally, churches must clearly indicate to emerging adults the relevancy of their church experience and help to guide them into an intimate and personal relationship with God. Finally, young adults who know and understand their purpose and who exercise their Holy Spirit given gifts will be more inclined to commit fully to God and the church.

Objectives

The objectives for the research study were to increase the number of emerging adults who are aware of their Holy Spirit given gifts and talents; increase the number of emerging adults who embrace and operate in their Holy Spirit-given gifts and talents; and to equip, empower and engage the participants in the research so that they would then be able to duplicate and bring about long-term viability and duplication of this research as leaders both within and outside of the church.

As an end product, a process for introducing college age individuals to theoretical foundation focused on Holy Spirit gifts, talents and abilities, complimented with mentoring and leadership development is now being taught to young adults. In addition, survey data through focus groups, and individual surveys and interviews was compiled as a resource for future young adult ministry.

Chapter 2

Research Foundations

A. **Biblical Foundations**

The biblical foundations focused on Jeremiah 1:4-10 and First Timothy 4-6. These scriptures explore Jeremiah's call to the office of prophet at a very young age and his ultimate commitment to God (through obedience). In Timothy, the researcher examines the mentoring relationship between Paul and Timothy, and Paul's admonition to Timothy that God and the council confirmed his gifts. Finally, an emphasis was placed on Timothy's unfailing commitment to the church and God.

The search through the Bible clearly revealed evidence that many individuals were consistently led away from their everyday lives to serve God in various capacities through encounters with the Holy Spirit. In some cases, they were both mentored and trained. In others, they were simply led of God. However, in all of these encounters, individuals were led to surrender themselves to a life of obedience to God, to practice and perfect the Holy Spirit gifts, talents and abilities that were activated within them, and to support those things dictated as important to God, primarily the church and its people. Countless individuals like Jeremiah, Elisha, Elijah, David, Timothy, Titus, Paul and a host of others, provide biblical examples of individuals who were handpicked by God to complete a specific service, at a specific time, for a specific purpose. This too has been my experience with God so while researching the biblical evidence of this path as being walked by many, this project became more informed and the research more justified. In First Corinthians 2:12, Paul substantiates the existence of these gifts and their initiation in individuals when he says, "Now we have received not the spirit of the world, but the Spirit that is from God, so that we may understand the gifts bestowed upon us by God." He goes further to say that while "there are a variety of gifts, services and activities; God activates them all through the manifestation of the Spirit for the common good." Additional support for the existence of these gifts also exists in First Corinthians 12:7-11, which states,

> To each is given the manifestation of the Spirit for the common good. To one is given through the Spirit the utterance of wisdom, and to another the utterance of knowledge according to the same Spirit, to another faith by the same Spirit, to another gifts of healing by the one Spirit, to another the working of miracles, to another prophecy, to another the discernment of spirits, to another various kinds of tongues, to another the interpretation of tongues. All these are activated by one and the same Spirit, who allots to each one individually just as the Spirit chooses (1 Corinthians 12:7-11).[16]

and Ephesians 4:11, where Paul goes further, detailing the variety of Spiritual Gifts bestowed upon individuals, "The gifts he gave were that some would be apostles, some prophets, some evangelists, some pastors, and teachers."

No matter the gift, spiritual experiences with God have long been understood to derive from the source of the Holy Spirit, the portion of God's spirit that is said to reside within each individual. Trinitarian terminology, which

---

[16] Biblical citations within the document are from the New Revised Standard Version unless otherwise noted, 1 Corinthians 12:7-11.

includes references to the Father, the Son and the Holy Spirit, serves as the ultimate source of godly wisdom, experience and insight. Tertullian, a theologian who was the son of a Roman centurion from North Africa, is credited with the terminology.[17] Born around 160 A.D., he converted to Christianity in 197 A.D., and it is in his writings that the Latin word *"trinity"* is first used to describe the relationship between the Father, Son, and Holy Spirit, whom he taught were "one God in three persons."[18] The focus shifts primarily to the Holy Spirit, however, when examining Holy Spirit and God-given gifts. Paul believed that the Holy Spirit indwells in an individual to: enable believers to live a righteous and faithful life by directing them to obedience; provide the stamp of God's ownership that then bears witness with an individual's own spirit; allow for miracles, signs and wonders to occur; and activate, pour out, and perfect spiritual gifts and talents in an individual for the purpose of service to God.[19] This description of the Holy Spirit's work within an individual is the impetus for gift activation and commitment to church, which is the focus of this research project.

There are many biblical instances in which those who describe being accosted by, assaulted by or even captivated by the Holy Spirit have indeed been

---

[17] Allan D. Menzies, *Latin Christianity, Its Founder, Tertullian*, vol. 3, *The Writings of the Fathers Down to AD 325* (Grand Rapids: T and T Clark), accessed August 1, 2012, http://www.ccel.org/ccel/schaff/anf03.toc.html#P334_131093.

[18] Ibid.

[19] Barry D. Smith, "The Holy Spirit in Pauline Theology," (lecture, The New Testament and its Context, Crandall University Religious Studies Program), accessed August 10, 2012. Http://www.abu.nb.ca/courses/NTIntro/Spirit7.htm.

converted, changed and realigned to commit to their God-given purpose in life. The existence of God-given gifts, talents and abilities and the central role of the Holy Spirit in activating them have been further substantiated in various biblical texts. While these actions take many forms, some heard the voice of God directly while individuals who were already serving God in a certain capacity confirmed others; the end result is the same. These encounters served to activate the Holy Spirit gifts within individuals, leading them to a stronger relationship with God and a greater commitment to the things of God, including church.

Two strong examples of this phenomenon occur within the biblical stories of Jeremiah in the Old Testament, and Timothy in the New Testament. While Jeremiah outlines the story of an individual accosted by God and led into service after activation of Holy Spirit gifts, Timothy tells the story of Holy Spirit gift activation through Holy Spirit affirmation and leadership development through Godly-appointed mentors and leaders. In both instances, however, God causes a bringing forth of Holy Spirit gifts that were already placed within an individual. In Jeremiah 1:5, God tells Jeremiah "Before I formed you in the womb, I knew you, and before you were born I consecrated you; I appointed you a prophet to the nations." This sets forth a divine commission for Jeremiah in which he has been predestined to share God's word. "The call to prophet was not simply the consequence of divine whim, but the expression of firm purpose."[20] He was created for his purpose well before he even understood it.

With Timothy, much of the indication that God called him is demonstrated through the words of his God-assigned mentor Paul. In First Timothy 4:14-16, Paul instructs Timothy not to forget the spiritual gift that is within him and which had been given to him "through prophecy with the laying on of hands by the council of elders." Biblical scripture indicates that Timothy's gifts included evangelism, preaching, teaching, and leadership, as outlined within First Timothy and Second Timothy. His concerns, therefore, are to be the concerns of God; namely standing for what is just and right and serving God's people.

The role envisaged for Timothy is clear throughout; Paul instructs him and he instructs others accordingly. It is implied that Timothy is Paul's "personal representative and emissary."[21] Thus, the discussion of Timothy and Paul will include an examination of the mentor relationship and how it affects commitment to church and God. Both texts clearly demonstrate the basic premise of the research; when Holy Spirit gifts are activated and properly directed, they can lead individuals into a stronger commitment to both the church and God.

---

[20] Peter C. Craigie, Page H. Kelley and Joel F. Drinkard, Jr., *Jeremiah 1-25*, vol. 26 *World Biblical Commentary* (Dallas, TX: Word Books, 1991), 580.

[21] J. Paul Sampley, Leander E. Keck and Abraham Smith, *The New Interpreter's Bible*, vol. 9, *A Commentary in Twelve Volumes* (Nashville, TN: Abingdon Press, 1994) 813.

The Book of Jeremiah is made up of the words of the prophet Jeremiah who was established during the reign of the last four kings of Judah.[22] While Jeremiah's age is not specifically given, it is thought that he was a young prophet, either a teenager or in his early twenties. According to biblical historians, his prophetic activity occurred during the last four decades of Judah's existence. While there is debate concerning the accuracy of the date for the beginning of Jeremiah's prophetic activity, "historically, the prophecy of Jeremiah begins in a time of glory, and ends in a time of judgment and disaster."[23] The book clearly chronicles the tragic events surrounding and following the Babylonian invasion of Judah, (597, 587, 4582 B.C.E.).[24] Dealing with the country's separation from God and the things of God, and their marriage to things that were far from godly, undoubtedly set the stage for a prophet who is said to have been one of the most sensitive to God's mission and most dedicated to serving God.

Jeremiah's prophetic words cover Judah during the critical years spanning the "golden age" of the Judean King Josiah (640-609 B.C.E.), the subsequent fall

---

[22] Thomas W. Overholt, *Harper Collins Bible Commentary* (New York, NY: Harper Collins Publishers, Inc., 1988), 538.

[23] J. Paul Sampley, Leander E. Keck and Abraham Smith, *The New Interpreter's Bible,* vol. 9, *A Commentary in Twelve Volumes* (Nashville, TN: Abingdon Press, 1994), 576.

[24] Kathleen M. O'Connor, "The Prophet Jeremiah and Exclusive Loyalty to God." *Interpretation* 59, no. 2:130-140, *ATLA Religion Database with ATLASerials*, EBSCO*host* (accessed March 19, 2013). http://search.ebscohost.com/login.aspx?direct=true&db=rfh&AN=ATLA0001455228&site=ehost-live.

and destruction of Jerusalem and the exile of the Judean population into captivity (597-586 B.C.E.).[25] They highlight Judah's broken covenant with God and God's judgment upon Judah, as well as the people's eventual return and restoration. "Every poem, narrative, sermon, or symbolic act of Jeremiah relates to the Babylonian invasions one way or another, announcing them, explaining them or offering hope for surviving them."[26] Some have even labeled this period as a "disaster" because those who were affected faced all-encompassing events with little support in the aftermath of the events, because both their institutions and their hopes were destroyed.[27]

> To grasp the overwhelming suffering and despair that must have followed the Babylonians invasions requires little historical imagination. After years of international intrigue and maneuvering, Babylonia troops twice invaded Jerusalem (597 and 587 B.C.E.) destroyed the king's palace, razed the temple, and deported some of the leading citizens to Babylon. The Babylonian army then occupied Judah and Jerusalem and a rebellion by some Judahites provoked a third invasion.[28]

This is the historical and social setting within which the prophet operated. It is easy, within this social context, to understand why the prophet spent much of his time alone and in despair. Daily disruption of life, the loss of stability in terms of government and religious leadership, the possible loss of livelihood for those

---

[25] Ibid.

[26] O'Connor, *"The Prophet Jeremiah and Exclusive Loyalty to God,"* 132.

[27] Ibid.

[28] Ibid.

living during this time period, and for those exiled, the loss of their homeland all worked together to create a tenuous, transitional, environment of both suffering and despair.[29] It is a setting in which turmoil permeates daily life in Judah and that is reflected in both the life of the prophet and the literary structure of the book.

    The book's brief introduction is reflective of the entire book in which little if any attention is given to presenting information in a chronological or sequential order.[30] The book of Jeremiah contains connected, but seemingly diverse and loosely organized content. It is interesting to note that Jeremiah's words echoed this literary pattern; indeed he felt very disconnected from the society that he lived in during this time. There seems not to have existed a pattern of organization within the entire work and the opening text initiates that pattern. Possibly the writers used this literary style to mirror the social situation at the time; the people of Judah were leading lives that were very much spiritually out of order. The biblical texts accuse them of "spiritual harlotry," defiling their relationship with God and choosing to forget what God had done for them in the past, and instead separating from God, (Jeremiah 3:1-2).

---

[29] Ibid.

[30] Thomas W. Overholt, *Harper Collins Bible Commentary: The Society of Bible Literature*, 538.

The book does not outline a specific historical period nor are the words of the prophet directly quoted.[31] It is loosely organized with no narrative, plot line or principles of organization, seemingly indicative of the social order at the time as well as Jeremiah's state of mind.[32] The book contains poetic oracles, biographical prose and sermons and prophetic utterances, and while some sections serve to employ one or the other of these literary forms, there is continuous comingling of these in many sections. The book also includes prophetic utterances and something that occurs in no other prophetic book "the personal complaint or lament of the prophet."[33] We are able to experience the pain, loss and spiritual upheaval that run through the veins of the prophet at the same time that the country is being torn apart and its people are being ravished, and to some extent, left to fend for themselves by God.

Jeremiah seems to be reacting emotionally due to the negative changes occurring in Judah. While Jeremiah was not a resident of Judah, he should have been very familiar with the activities occurring within that city since he was a resident of Anathoth, a town located three miles northeast of Jerusalem and bordering Judah.[34] Some scholars believe that Jeremiah was born in 627 B.C.E.

---

[31] Ibid.

[32] Ibid.

[33] Ibid.

[34] J.F. Walvoord, R. B. Zuck, and Dallas Theological Seminary, *The Bible Knowledge Commentary: An Exposition of the Scriptures* (Wheaton, IL: Victor Books, 1985), 157.)

and began his prophetic ministry in 609 B.C.E., following the death of King Josiah.[35] Biblical text, however, indicates that he began his ministry in 627 B.C.E. (Jeremiah 25:3) and prophesied until after deportation and the flight of the major group of Judeans to Egypt.[36] If this is so, Jeremiah's ministry spanned forty-one years, up until the people of Israel went into exile.

Jeremiah's home was one of the cities that had been allotted by Joshua to priests and Jeremiah was descended from the priestly line of Aaron.[37] While priests may have had little power prior to exile, they would have held a level of reverence toward God as priestly servants of God. Their position dictated that they would have had some spiritual understanding of God's covenant with his people, and the consequences of breaking that covenant since they served as ministers to the people. In addition, one can assume some level of training and mentoring also occurred as part of the preparation to serve in the priesthood. However, his priestly lineage "seems only to have increased his isolation and enhanced the danger to him."[38]

---

[35] Ibid.

[36] Ibid.

[37] Ibid.

[38] Patrick D. Miller, *Jeremiah*, vol. 6, *The New Interpreter's Bible, A Commentary in Twelve Volumes* (Nashville, TN: Abingdon Press, 1994), 573.

There is not much biblical text concerning Jeremiah's call to the office of prophet. The small amount of text speaks briefly to Jeremiah's biological history, and the extent of his prophetic service to God. Jeremiah 1:1-3 provides the details of Jeremiah's life, indicating his lineage, his city of origin, and the length of his service as a prophet of God. This small amount of information is set forth quickly before the text moves into a discussion of the call on the prophet's life. Possibly, the goal is to focus on the work of the prophet and not who he was or where he was from. Since he did not have much history, that information is unimportant except to suggest his prior connection to God. It also sets the example that anyone can be used powerfully of God.

The prophet's call is initiated in Jeremiah 1:4-5 when it is revealed that the "word of the Lord" came to Jeremiah. "Before I formed you in the womb I knew you, and before you were born I consecrated you: I appointed you a prophet to the nations." Clearly, Jeremiah had been created to serve God during a specific season and for a specific purpose and with specific gifts, though they had yet to be fully activated. The word "knew" traditionally meant much more than intellectual knowledge. It had been used to convey the sense of a close and personal relationship during this time period. When God says that he "knew" Jeremiah before he was even formed in the womb, it demonstrates that he was designed, developed and set aside to be a spokesman for God to Israel. Jeremiah had been set apart, "consecrated," as the text reads, sanctified and made holy for God's use and purpose (Jeremiah 1:5). In his lineage with the priesthood one can assume that Jeremiah had already been consecrated, but God mentions this to serve a larger purpose of assuring Jeremiah of his readiness to serve in this additional capacity.

In 1:6 Jeremiah answers God's call with self-doubt. He tells God that he does not know how to speak. He attributes this to his age and status as a boy. As mentioned earlier there is some debate as to Jeremiah's age, but in this instance Jeremiah seems to be hinting that he is still "young" in wisdom and the knowledge of God, not in actual years. Coming from a position or residing within a lineage of priests, he would have had some sensitivity to his being "young" in ministry. However, God answers Jeremiah's objections with a clear response that is biblically substantiated in Romans 8:26 "likewise the Spirit helps us in our weakness…" and by Romans 8:30 "And those whom he predestined he also called; and those whom he called he also justified; and those whom he justified he also glorified." God then puts his hand out and touches the young prophet's mouth, sealing the deal and calling forth the God-given gift, saying, "Now I have put my words in your mouth. See, today I appoint you Over nations and kingdoms, to pluck up and pull down, to destroy and To overthrow, to build and to plant" (Jeremiah 1:10). There is no more discussion. Jeremiah has been called, his gifts are initiated, and he is empowered and equipped by God. He obviously accepts his call immediately, because within the very next scripture he speaks of the Word of the Lord that came to him (Jeremiah 1:11). God has explained the call on his life, assured him that he has already been consecrated and appointed, explained that his success would rely primarily on his obedience to speak the words that God would provide and not his own fortitude, and provided Jeremiah the security of knowing that God would always be with him and would protect him. Jeremiah needed only to be fearless, speak what was given to him to speak when it was given to him, and to go where he was sent.

Thus begins Jeremiah's journey into a life of service to God prompted by the initiation of previously dormant Holy Spirit gifts placed in him by God, and maintained through obedience to the direction and guidance of God, and submission to the righteousness of God. While Jeremiah had indeed lived a life that was connected to God in some manner prior to his call to serve as a prophet, biblical text suggest that the latter extent and level of commitment to God and the church, far outweighed anything that came prior to his call to the prophetic. Greater sacrifice, greater commitment, greater suffering, and greater obedience were essential parts of his later call to serve God.

The Pastoral Epistles are where we find the next example of an individual who has been called by God and prepared to serve through the activation of their Holy Spirit-given gifts and talents. The letters that appear in the books of Timothy and Titus are part of the "Pastoral Epistles," called so because they focus primarily on the internal life, governance and behavior of Christian communities, specifically those within the Pauline mission field of churches. They include First and Second Timothy, and First and Second Titus. The letters are so grouped because they share a similar vocabulary and style, subject matter and theology, as well as a similar purpose, which is to preserve the Pauline message.[39] They resemble administrative letters from a supervisor to a subordinate, indicative of a mentoring relationship, and while they did not appear in the earliest collection of Pauline letters, they have been included from the late second century on. Each letter is considered a "hortatory" meaning that it includes exhortation in an effort to address the behavior of individual members of the church.[40]

The specific letter for primary examination includes that written by Paul in First Timothy. It was composed during a period in which the behavior and doctrine of certain teachers within the Pauline ministry community had destabilized the Christian community, both doctrinally and socially.[41] Scriptures written in other books of the Pastoral Epistles such as Philippians 2:12-15 and Colossians. 2:8, while less stringent and less corrective, do indicate that this was a time of faith challenges, infighting by various factors within the community, competition and challenges to the basic principles of Christianity. Each Pauline

---

[39] Thomas W. Overholt. *Harper Collins Bible Commentary: The Society of Bible Literature*, 1137.

[40] Ibid.

[41] Ibid.

community seemed to have had its own challenges and the letters are tailored to address those challenges.

There is some debate concerning authorship of the letters. While the letters are intended for churches within the Pauline mission field, the real author is never mentioned.[42] Many scholars contend that these letters were not written by Paul, but were written after his death, following the custom at the time of borrowing Paul's name and theology for authoritative purposes, to address a crisis occurring at the Second-Century church.[43] They base this position on the belief that there is uncharacteristic vocabulary and style contained within the letters. Other evidence maintains that Paul is the author and these individuals attach a date of A.D. 62-66 to their origination, at least eighty years after Paul's three-year stay in Ephesus.[44] Whether Paul produced them are not the letters are clearly indicative of Pauline theology and Christian beliefs maintained by Paul.

The recipient of the letters in Timothy is said to have been the son of a marriage between a Jewish mother and a Greek speaking Jewish father.[45] His grandmother and then mother evidently grounded Timothy in the faith, as

---

[42] Ibid.

[43] Ibid.

[44] "Summary of the Book of 1 Timothy," *BibleStudy Tools*, accessed November 12, 2013, http://www.biblestudytools.com/1-timothy/.

[45] D.R. Wood and I. H. Marshall, New Bible Dictionary (Downers Grove, IL: InterVarsity Press, 1996).

mentioned in Second Timothy 1:4-5. He was a native of Lystra, a city visited by Paul several times and where Paul suffered persecution. Timothy must not only have been familiar with Christianity, but also had witnessed the responses of those who rejected that word and undoubtedly, this nervousness must have been a part of his hesitancy to lead at Ephesus. In a previous visit, Paul had converted Timothy's mother Eunice.[46] It is not clear when Timothy became a Christian, but it is reasonable to assume that he was an early convert of Paul's, as Paul indicates that he witnessed his sufferings at Lystra (2 Timothy 3:11). Paul also had an affinity for Timothy evidenced because he chose him to travel with him, providing Timothy with an opportunity to be mentored and trained for the future that he was unaware of. Timothy was with Paul when he evangelized at Macedonia and Achaia (Acts 17:14-15 and 18:5) and was also with him during his preaching ministry at Ephesus (Acts 19:22). He traveled with Paul from Ephesus to Macedonia, to Corinth, back to Macedonia, and to Asia Minor.[47] He was with Paul during the apostle's first imprisonment and following Paul's release, but he eventually was asked to stay at Ephesus to deal with the problems there, while Paul went on to Macedonia.

---

[46] John Rutherfurd, *International Standard Bible Encyclopedia,* Biblios, accessed May 1, 2013, http://bibleencyclopedia.com/timothy.htm.

[47] "Through Macedonia and Greece," *BibleStudy Tools,* accessed May 1, 2013, http://www.biblestudytools.com/bible/passage.aspx?q=acts+20:1-6.

Paul's closeness to and admiration of Timothy are seen in Paul's naming him as the co-sender of six of his letters (Second Corinthians, Philippians, Colossians, 1, 2 Thessalonians and Philemon) and in his speaking highly of him to the Philippians, "I hope in the Lord Jesus to send Timothy to you soon, so that I may be cheered by news of you. I have no one like him who will be genuinely concerned for your welfare" (Philippians 2:19-20). Paul showed a great respect and love for Timothy and made references to him as "his beloved and faithful son in the Lord" (First Corinthians 4:17) and "my true child in faith" (First Timothy 1:2). He calls Timothy a "man of God" (First Timothy 6:11), which is considered one of the greatest titles that could be bestowed upon him since it would seem that everyone who has the Spirit of God within them, would seek to claim that title. Thus, while Jeremiah, as discussed above, may not have had a clearly defined mentor to walk with him, Timothy obviously had this in Paul. Thus, in addition to providing a clear example of how recognition of Holy Spirit gifts can bring forth a commitment to church and God, this text also emphasizes the importance of mentoring; part of the recipe used in the researcher's project to reach the desired outcome. The relationship between Timothy and Paul provides a clear example of how mentoring can inform and help to create commitment to God and the church.

The mentoring relationship between Paul and Timothy initially evolves due to an affinity that Paul obviously held toward Timothy, even at the initial meeting. At the onset, Paul says that he saw something of value in Timothy, and he expresses this in Second Timothy 1:5 when he says, "I am reminded of your sincere faith, a faith that lived first in your grandmother Lois and your mother Eunice and now, I am sure lives in you." Paul clearly believes that particular Holy Spirit gifts have been bestowed upon Timothy, and later, he seems to accept it as his job not only to mentor Timothy, but to indeed prepare Timothy to succeed him in his own work. Throughout the Bible there are references to Timothy as a close worker with Paul, who could be trusted to be dispatched to churches to represent Paul as needed. Paul also refers to Timothy as his "co-worker" (Romans 16:21) and his "son," (Philippians 2:22) indicating a close personal and professional relationship between the two. Later, he even refers to Timothy as "my beloved and faithful child in the Lord" indicating a "spiritual fatherhood," a frequent component of the mentoring relationship that entails teaching, raising and advising those placed under your spiritual care (1 Cor. 4:17). Paul clearly sees Timothy as an inheritor of his own knowledge and work, and thus his mantle, and further, expects him to pass on all that he has learned in the same way (2 Tim 2:2). In essence, Paul not only acknowledges and confirms the Holy Spirit gifts within Timothy, but he also sees himself as a mentor to him, eventually helping him to develop and use those gifts in his service to God, and to prepare to become a mentor, in his own right. It is obvious that the mentoring part of the relationship, therefore, ultimately served to undergird and spearhead Timothy's eventual dedication to both God and the church. This invaluable contribution to the young man's ministry cannot be doubted or diminished.

While Paul clearly saw Timothy as a mentee, he also focused on developing the professional aspect of Timothy's life, understanding the call on Timothy's life; that he had been consecrated and set apart for the work that he was to accomplish (1 Tim. 1:18 and 4:14). Again, he has already ignited Timothy's gifts through the laying on of hands, "I remind you, to rekindle the gift of God that is within you through the laying on of my hands," so the focus is now on developing both the gifts within Timothy, as well as the necessary leadership abilities (2 Tim. 1:6). Paul clearly knew and understood the powerful call that was placed upon Timothy's life, and granted many opportunities for Timothy to be successful such as placing him at Ephesus and Corinth.

Unlike Jeremiah, there is no indication that God spoke to Timothy directly concerning his Holy Spirit gifts, but clearly Paul and the religious leadership believed they received confirmation of Timothy's call. His authority is also clearly underlined by various references to a particular commissioning event that contained three elements: the giving of his charisma, that is presumably by the Spirit, a prophecy (prophetic utterance); and the laying on of hands by the presbytery."[48] The letters in Timothy include many instances of Paul's references

---

[48] J. Paul Sampley, Leander E. Keck and Abraham Smith, *The New Interpreter's Bible,* vol. 9, *A Commentary in Twelve Volumes* (Nashville, TN: Abingdon Press, 1994), 814.

to God "equipping and preparing of Timothy to successfully complete the task at hand." While the letters offer guidance, they also clearly offer encouragement and recognition of Timothy's God-given abilities. A clear example occurs in First Timothy 4:14-15, "Do not neglect the gift that is in you, which was given to you through prophecy with the laying on of hands by the council of elders."

Scripture provides that not only was Timothy believed to have been called by God to complete his assigned tasks, he had also been fully equipped and prepared to recognize success with the comingling of the various gifts and abilities that had already been placed within him. God's word dictates that everyone who is called by God, chooses to accept that call, and follows a course of obedience to that call shall be equipped to serve (Romans 8:28). So, while Timothy may have wavered in his faith in the third chapter, at some point he expressed a desire to leave Ephesus, it is clear that Paul had full confidence that he was fit for the task. In spite of the fact that Timothy, at this age, is filled with self-doubt and he is engaging in a constant search for identity.

Paul writes these letters to Timothy to instruct Timothy to oppose the false doctrines that Paul had previously urged him to oppose (First Timothy 1:3), to give Timothy instructions needed to fight a strong fight (First Timothy 1:18-19), to instruct Timothy on how God's people should conduct themselves (First Timothy 3:14-15), and to provide input as to how he should conduct his pastoral ministry (First Timothy 4:1-6:19). The activation and fulfillment of Timothy's

God-given call is most clearly spoken to through the final purpose of Paul's letters; instruction on how Timothy should conduct his ministry. First and foremost, Paul admonishes Timothy not to forget that he has been empowered by God to succeed. Paul says, "Do not neglect the gift that is in you." This "gift" possibly included Timothy's aptitude for teaching and preaching, along with an ability to understand the gospel and discern error.[49] The easiest way for Timothy to neglect his gift would have been to fail to acknowledge or employ it as the God-given means to successfully complete his assignment. Paul is trying to encourage Timothy to take his attention away from his own shortcomings, and turn it to God, who equips and perfects those whom he calls (Romans 8:30).

Next, Paul reminds Timothy that God did indeed call him to this task, and that his call was not only witnessed by others, but seconded by those within the highest positions of the church, the "council of leaders," or the priests (1 Tim. 4:14). Paul must remind Timothy that if both God and those who lead the church say that he has been equipped and consecrated for this task, he should be careful not to question it or to respond in a careless manner toward it. Confirmation and clarification of not only Holy Spirit-gifting, but one's ability to succeed at that task, are very necessary components of leading individuals to commit to church and God, especially young adults. During this time in life, there is a strong focus

---

[49] T. D. Lea and H. P. Griffin, *The New American Commentary* (Nashville, TN: Broadman and Holman Publishers, 1992).

on identity and nervousness about accomplishment that must be addressed. Therefore, the researcher needed to reaffirm the participants concerning their spiritual gifts and their capacity to use them. Just as with Paul this often takes the form of positive affirmation and opportunities to complete tasks associated with a particular gifting. Paul does this with Timothy, providing confidence about his abilities.

The "laying on of hands" as referenced within First Timothy 4:15, is indicative of the succession of ministerial authority. Paul states that both he and the elders laid hands on Timothy, indicating that there indeed was agreement on the gifts and talents within the young man. Next, Paul tells Timothy to "put these things into practice, devote yourself to them, so that all may see your progress." Here Paul is telling Timothy to live a spiritual life, above reproach, and demonstrative of Christian character. In an earlier scripture within the same text, First Timothy 4:12-13, Paul also has admonished Timothy to live above reproach when he says, "Let no one despise your youth, but set the believers an example in speech and conduct, in love, in faith, in purity. Until I arrive, give attention to the public reading of scripture, to exhorting, to teaching." While he tells Timothy not to allow others to question him because of his age, acceptable estimates put Timothy's age at between thirty and thirty-five, but some at Ephesus would still consider this to be young.[50] Paul is also reminding Timothy that his age is not his limitation and that if he embraces the God-given talents within him, he can and will succeed.

In at least three scriptures, First Timothy 1:18, First Timothy 4:14 and Second Timothy 1:6, Paul reminds Timothy of his call and the gifts, abilities and authorities contained within it. Obviously, Paul does not take this lightly. Instead, he states that he is an apostle called by Christ at least twice (1 Tim. 1:1-2 and Romans 1:1). His letters indicate that he understands both the capacity of God-given gifts, talents and abilities, and the burden of such. "An apostle does not undertake a commission in obedience to his own whim. Literally, he is 'one sent'."[51] Simply stated, Paul clearly understands the burdens, trials, challenges, and complications faced by Timothy because he himself has been called to serve God, and he has employed the necessary means to be successful in that endeavor so he is the perfect person to teach those things to Timothy. Timothy has not only been equipped with God-given gifts and talents, but he has been sent one who can guide, direct and remind him of what has been placed inside of him and for what purpose. Timothy provides an excellent example of one who acknowledges his God-given gifts, talents and abilities initiated through the Holy Spirit and makes a

---

[50] Ibid.

[51] George Buttrick, "Timothy: The Divine Commission," vol. 11, *The Interpreter's Bible Library in Twelve Volumes* (Nashville, TN: Abingdon Press, 1955).

conscious decision to serve God, in spite of the trials and tribulations. God equips Timothy and Timothy fully submits himself to God.

Both Jeremiah and Timothy clearly provide emphatic proof that individuals can and are called to serve God. Other biblical examples include Isaiah, whose mouth was touched by God to call him into service (Isaiah 6:4-9), Samuel who eventually responded to his call after repeatedly hearing his name called by the voice of God (First Samuel 3), Ezekiel who was moved into action by a vision of God (Ezekiel 1:1), and Elisha, who was led into service by a servant of God, the prophet Elijah (First King 19:19). These are only a sampling, but collectively they paint a full picture of how an individual can truly carry a Holy Spirit gift that when ignited or initiated, causes a spiritual encounter that leads to commitment to God and the things of God, including the church.

Scripture, too, supports this contention. The most common text is First Corinthians 12:7-11, in which Paul not only acknowledges that gifts are given through the Holy Spirit, but goes further to mention exactly what some of those gifts are. Romans 12 contains a reference to spiritual gifts and provides a brief explanation of how they are disseminated. First Peter admonishes individuals to be good stewards of whatever gifts that they have received. Finally Ephesians 4:11emphatically states that God gave gifts to God's people as God ascended up to heaven. All these texts give credence to the fact that God indeed places gifts within individuals, activates those gifts at a preordained time, sends others to support and fully equip those who are walking in their gifting and finally, causes individuals to develop a stronger commitment to God and the church.

B. **Historical Foundations**

If history is an indication, individuals who choose to accept and exercise their God-given gifts, talent and abilities, tend to gain a stronger and more focused dedication to the things of God. There are many historical figures that testify, through autobiographical stories and oratory accounts that they experienced moments of spiritual clarity during which the Holy Spirit provided a lucid understanding of how they were to serve God. In describing these accounts, these individuals say that those moments took many forms. Some say that they clearly heard voices telling them what their life work should be. Others experienced visions that led them to an understanding of what they were to do, and some claim sudden conversions that came upon them quickly. All of the accounts describe an awakening of sorts; a moment of clarity and closeness to God, enabled through the Holy Spirit, during which the focus of their lives was changed dramatically. Each testimony supports the contention that the activation of an individual's Holy Spirit given gifts, talents and abilities may result in a greater commitment to both church and God.

Spiritual experiences with God have long been understood to derive from the source of the Holy Spirit, the portion of God's spirit that is said to reside within each individual. The Trinity terminology, which includes the Father, the Son and the Holy Spirit, serves as the ultimate source of godly wisdom, experience and insight. Tertullian, a theologian who was the son of a Roman centurion from North Africa, is credited with the terminology.[52] Born around 160 AD, he converted to Christianity in 197 A.D., after receiving an education in literature and theology.[53] It is in Tertullian's writings that we first find the Latin word "trinity" to describe the relationship between the Father, Son, and Holy Spirit, whom he taught were "one God in three persons."[54]

When examining spiritual or God-given gifts, the focus shifts primarily to the element of the Holy Spirit within the Trinity. Although the concept of the Holy Spirit was not clearly understood, it did play a role in the formation of the early church and early Christianity. According to Alister E. McGrath in *"Christian Theology: An Introduction,"* the early church found itself puzzled by the Spirit and unable to make much in the way of theological sense of this area of the doctrine of God."[55] McGrath goes on to say that while there were those who focused on the activity of the Holy Spirit during this time like Montanus, a

---

[52] Allan D. Menzies, *Latin Christianity, Its Founder, Tertullian,*" vol. 3, *The Writings of the Fathers Down to AD 325* (Grand Rapids, MI: T and T Clark) accessed November 10, 2013.

[53] Ibid.

[54] Ibid.

[55] Alister E. McGrath, *Christian Theology: An Introduction* (Kings College, NY: John Wiley and Sons, Ltd. 2011), 228.

religious leader of the *lluminati*, "there was a relative absence of discussion related to the role of the Holy Spirit during the first three centuries of the church. Therefore, the full divinity of the Spirit took place at a relatively late stage."[56] One of the most significant contributors to the development of the theology of the Holy Spirit, according to McGrath, was Augustine. He regarded the Holy Spirit as the unifying bond between the Father and the Son, and between God and Believers. Augustine believed that the Holy Spirit forged bonds of unity between believers, upon which the unity of the church ultimately depended.[57]

Christian tradition generally lists the work of the Holy Spirit as focused in three broad areas including revelation, salvation, and the Christian life.[58] According to Christian tradition, the task of the Holy Spirit is to reveal God's truth and make it known to humanity.[59] The Holy Spirit is also said to be involved with human response to that revelation, essentially leading to faith and serving to sanctify the human spirit, making humanity more like God.[60] Additionally, Christian theology often adds that the Holy Spirit serves to make God real during

---

[56] Ibid., 230.

[57] Ibid., 231.

[58] Ibid.

[59] Ibid.

[60] Ibid., 232.

personal and corporate worship and devotion, as well as shaping and sustaining the Christian community, fostering its witness to the world.[61]

Pauline Theology clearly dictates the purposes of the Holy Spirit. Paul believed that the Holy Spirit indwells in an individual to: enable believers to live a righteous and faithful life by directing them to obedience; provide the stamp of God's ownership that then bears witness with an individual's own spirit; allow for miracles, signs and wonders to occur; and to activate, pour out and perfect spiritual gifts and talents in an individual for the purpose of service to God.[62] Further, Pauline Theory states that the Holy Spirit has been conferred on all believers in Christ, and serves to help with obedience to the law, as prophesied by Ezekiel.[63] This description of the Holy Spirit's work in an individual most closely relates to the process of gift activation. Regardless of which description is examined, it is clear that the Holy Spirit plays an integral role in the spiritual development of Christians. In addition, it is obvious that it can serve to activate the God-given gifts, talents and abilities imbued within an individual, instructing and guiding them toward a particular "call" or specific work that they were ultimately created for.

---

[61] Ibid.

[62] Barry D. Smith, "The Holy Spirit in Pauline Theology," (lecture, The New Testament and its Context, Crandall University Religious Studies Program), accessed August 10, 2012. Http://www.abu.nb.ca/courses/NTIntro/Spirit7.htm.

[63] Ibid.

Spiritual gifts, talents and abilities, or gifts of the Holy Spirit, are those abilities and skills bestowed upon an individual by God and activated by the Holy Spirit, according to Father William Saunders in the article, *"Gifts of the Holy Spirit."* Saunders describes these gifts as supernatural gifts operating in a supernatural mode or manner that are present within the person as long as the individual remains in a state of sanctifying grace.[64] He further states that these gifts help individuals share "in the very life and nature of God, now in this life and for eternal life.[65] In his text, Summa Theological I-II, Thomas Aquinas states that,

Human virtues perfect man insofar as man is naturally moved by reason in the things that he does within or without. Higher perfections must therefore be in man, by which he is disposed to be moved by God. And these perfections are called gifts, not only because they are infused by God, but also because by them, man is disposed and made more ready to be moved by the divine inspiration.[66]

Aquinas also stated that man could dwell within a realm of higher perfection under which he is moved by God. Further, the movements by God, which surface when individuals begin to work in spiritual gifting, are both imbued by God and prepare man to be moved by divine inspiration.

---

[64] William Saunders, "Gifts of the Holy Spirit," *Arlington Catholic Herald*, Republished by the Catholic Education Resource Center, 2003, accessed March 16, 2013, http://www.catholiceducation.org/articles/religion/re0451.html.

[65] Ibid.

[66] Thomas Aquinas, *"Summa Theological Part I-II."* q.68, a. from The Complete American Edition, Translated by Fathers of the English Dominican Province (New York: Benzinger Brothers) 2006, accessed March 17, 2013, http://www.gutenberg.org/cache/epub/17897/pg17897.html.

John Wesley, founder of Methodism, not only supported the existence of these gifts, but he went further to assert that not only did the gifts of the Holy Spirit exist; contrary to what some believed, they were just as relevant for the churches of his day, as they were for churches in past ages. Wesley claimed to have experienced them and he went so far as to use his writings to define them, describe them and to defend them;

> It does not appear that these extraordinary gifts of the Holy Ghost were common in the church for more than two or three centuries. We seldom hear of them after that fatal period when the Emperor Constantine called himself a Christian, and from a vain imagination of promoting the Christian cause thereby heaped riches, and power, and honour, upon the Christians in general; but in particular upon the Christian clergy. From this time they almost totally ceased; very few instances of the kind were found. The cause of this was not (as has been vulgarly supposed,) "because there was no more occasion for them," because all the world was become Christian. This is a miserable mistake; not a twentieth part of it was then nominally Christian. The real cause was, "the love of many," almost of all Christians, so called, was "waxed cold." The Christians had no more of the Spirit of Christ than the other Heathens. The Son of Man, when he came to examine his Church, could hardly "find faith upon earth." This was the real cause why the extraordinary gifts of the Holy Ghost were no longer to be found in the Christian Church -- because the Christians were turned Heathens again, and had only a dead form left.[67]

Wesley asserts that these "gifts are still accessible to individuals who choose to turn back to God in love and obedience."[68] Even with the many individuals who

---

[67] Edward Purkey, ed. "*The Sermons of John Wesley-Sermon 89: The More Excellent Way.*" (Wesley Center for Applied Theology at Northwest Nazarene University, 1999), accessed March 24, 2013, http://wesley.nnu.edu/john-wesley/the-sermons-of-john-wesley-1872-edition/sermon-89-the-more-excellent-way/.

[68] Ibid.

have affirmed and supported the existence of God-given gifts, talents and abilities, there is still debate as to their existence in contemporary society. Those who would contend that these gifts and talents existed within the early church during biblical times, also suggests that they no longer exist as part of today's church. Julie M. Douglas in *"Reflections on Divine Revelation and Personal Encounter with the Lord,"* says one reason for this is that for many people, God has become so remote that they no longer hear the voice of God.[69] The rationale for this, according to Douglas is that "God is viewed as so transcendent and almighty that there could not possibly be communication between God and mere human beings."[70]

History, however, seems to fall on the side of not only the existence of these gifts, but also the effect of them on individual lives. It appears that those who have either sought or embraced communion with the Holy Spirit, have indeed been converted, changed and realigned to their purpose in life. The existence of God-given gifts, talents and abilities and the central role of the Holy Spirit in activating them have been further substantiated in various biographical and autobiographical texts. Many claim that indeed a Holy Spirit encounter served

---

[69] Julie M. Douglas, "Reflections on Divine Revelation and Personal Encounter with the Lord." *AFER* 42, Issue 3-4 (June-Aug.), 151. *ATLA Religion Database with ATLASerials*, EBSCO*host*, accessed March 11, 2012, http://search.ebscohost.com/login.aspx?direct=true&db=rfh&AN=ATLA0001281173&site=ehost-live/.

[70] Ibid., 151.

to activate the special abilities within them, led them to their purpose in life and propelled them to a stronger commitment to God's people. St. Augustine of Hippo and St. Francis of Assisi both described hearing voices that made clear what their life work should be. St. Teresa of Avila said that she experienced a vision of Christ that caused her so much grief, that it changed her life forever. Each described a spiritual encounter that activated something new in them that changed their lives forever.

St. Augustine was one of many historical figures whose memoirs detail a spiritual encounter that dramatically affected the course of his life. A Fourth Century philosopher, and eventual bishop of Hippo Regius (Algeria) of the Roman province of Africa, Augustine was born on November 13, 354 in Africa and died August 28, 430.[71] Today, he is considered a "father of the church whose writings served to help develop Western Christianity and philosophy.[72] However, before his spiritual conversion, he had chosen an altogether different course and did not even abide in his Christian roots.

As a young child, Augustine received a Christian education and his mother had him signed with the cross.[73] This served to indicate the he was a Christian.

---

[71] *Internet Encyclopedia of Philosophy,* s.v. "Augustine," accessed April 12, 2012. http://www.iep.utm.edu/augustin/.

[72] *The American Heritage College Dictionary*, 3rd ed., s.v. "St. Augustine," (Boston, MA: Houghton Mifflin Publishing Company, 1992), 91.

[73] *Catholic Encyclopedia*, s.v. "St. Augustine," accessed April 12, 2012, http://www.newadvent.org/cathen/02084a/htm.

Once when very ill, he asked for baptism, but when the danger passed, he chose not to receive the sacrament.[74] As an adult, Augustine chose to leave the church to follow the Manichaean religion, which was then actively carried on in Africa. He was attracted to Manicheans because he was "enticed by the promise of free philosophy, unbridled by faith and the hope of finding a scientific explanation of nature."[75] Manichaean's felt at liberty to criticize the scriptures, especially the Old Testament, with perfect freedom; and they held chastity and self-denial in honor.[76] The prayer, which Augustine is said to have claimed as being in his heart during that time, reads, "Lord, give me chastity and temperance, but not now," and it is said to be symbolic of the attitudes of many of the Manicheans.[77] Augustine held firmly to these beliefs for nine years, during which time he scorned the sacraments of the church, and held frequent disputes with Catholic believers.[78]

However, in the summer of 386A.D. he was inspired and moved by a story about the life of St. Anthony of the Desert that focused on the monastic life and

---

[74] Ibid.

[75] Ibid.

[76] *Internet Encyclopedia of Philosophy,* s.v. "Augustine," accessed April 12, 2012. http://www.iep.utm.edu/augustin/.

[77] Ibid.

[78] Ibid.

64

St. Anthony's conquest over self that was won under its inspiration.[79] Augustine then began to ponder how he, with all of his learning, could still be held captive by the flesh.[80] This began the start of his conversion. While sitting away and pondering these thoughts, Augustine is said to have heard a voice coming from a neighboring home. It was the voice of a child that repeated the words, "take up and read" in Latin. Augustine took this as a heavenly indication and he picked up a copy of St. Paul's Epistle to the Romans, specifically chapters 12 through 15, where Paul outlines how the gospel transforms Believers and the Believer's resulting behavior. He focused on Romans 13:13-14, which he received as a decisive message sent to his soul, and his resolve was taken.[81] "No further would I read, nor did I need; for instantly, as the sentence ended – by a light, as it were, of security infused into my heart – all the gloom of doubt vanished away."[82]

He was convinced that the Lord had spoken to him and all of his doubt about the Christian faith was absolved. As a result of this spiritual encounter, Augustine chose to break completely from his old life. He gave up his position, requested baptism and among other things, began to record his thoughts and ideas in support of the Christian faith resulting in two of his most famous works,

---

[79] J.G. Pilkington, trans., *The Confessions* (Peabody, MS: Hendrickson Publishers, 1989).

[80] Ibid.

[81] Ibid.

[82] Ibid.

Confessions and *City of God* and going so far as to speak out against his past religious affiliations. Though his list of efforts under the auspices of Christianity are long, more generally he dedicated his life to his Christian faith by selling his inheritance, establishing the first monastery in Africa, becoming an ordained presbyter and later preaching to candidates for baptism.[83]

For St. Francis of Assisi, the issue of social justice was an instrumental element within the spiritual conversion that led him to dedicate himself to Christ. Though his total conversion occurred after several spiritual encounters that early planted a desire for the spiritual life within him, an instance of hearing the voice of God propelled him quickly into his call and brought forth the gifts, talents and concern for the poor that dictated his life.[84]

Born to a wealthy cloth merchant at Assisi in Umbria in 1181 or 1182, St. Francis seemed to be a spoiled young man, by all accounts. He had everything and he chose to enjoy it.[85] Even at that time, though he enjoyed life to the fullest, he is said to have shown sympathy for the poor.[86]

St. Francis' true spiritual conversion seems to have begun at the age of twenty-two, soon after he was released as a prisoner of the war between Assisi

---

[83] *Internet Encyclopedia of Philosophy,* s.v. "Augustine," accessed April 12, 2012. http://www.iep.utm.edu/augustin/.

[84] *Catholic Encyclopedia: Catholic Online,* s.v. "St. Francis of Assisi-Saints and Angels," accessed April 10, 2013, http://www.catholic.org/encyclopedia/view.php?id=4829.

[85] Ibid.
[86] Ibid., 1.

and Perugia. A low fever that he contracted while a prisoner made him begin to think about eternity, and when he arose from bed, he was "disgusted with himself and unsatisfied with the world."[87] St. Francis then chose a military career, but details of his life suggest that the night before he was to leave, he had a dream in which he saw a vast hall hung with amour all marked with the cross. He then heard a voice say, "These, are for you and your soldiers," and that convinced him that he would be a great prince.[88] However, a second illness stopped him as he was leaving, and another dream directed him to return home, which he did.[89] St. Francis then began to seek direction from God about his call through prayer and solitude.

The first recorded instance of his spiritual conversion, or at least a change in thought, occurred when he met a leper on a road while he was in Rome. Though initially disgusted by the leper, St. Francis eventually embraced the man and gave him all of the money that he had. Historians mark this as the beginning of his change of spirit.[90] Later, he emptied his purse at the tomb of St. Peter, and

---

[87] Ibid.

[88] *Catholic Encyclopedia: Catholic Online*, s.v. "St. Francis of Assisi-Saints and Angels," accessed April 10, 2013, http://www.catholic.org/encyclopedia/view.php?id=4829.

[89] Schaff, *History of the Christian Church*.

[90] Ibid., 2.

exchanged clothes with a poor beggar, spending the rest of the day fasting among the rest of the beggars at the door of the basilica.[91]

Once he returned home, St. Francis began to spend his time at chapels, most often at St. Damian, a barely furnished and crumbling chapel served by a sole priest. At one point while in prayer, Francis is said to have heard a voice, presumably that of God, which said, "Go, Francis, and repair my house, which as you see is falling." He immediately took goods from his father and gave them to the priest.[92] As a result he was mocked as a madman and dragged home by his father, beaten, bound and locked in a dark closet.

His mother later released him during his father's absence. St. Francis then renounced his filial obligation in public and this was the fullness of his conversion, as he publicly testified, "Up to this point, I have called Pietro Bernardone father, but now I desire to serve God and to say nothing else than, "Our Father which art in heaven."[93]

After this very public scene, Francis was devoted to the religious life. He dressed scantily and lived among the lepers, washing their sores.[94] He also fully

---

[91] Ibid.

[92] Ibid.

[93] Ibid.

[94] *Catholic Encyclopedia: Catholic Online,* s.v. "St. Francis of Assisi-Saints and Angels."

restored the St. Damian chapel, begging for stones on the city streets.[95] In 1209 his conversion was complete when he heard a voice that said, "Preach, the kingdom of heaven is at hand, heal the sick, cleanse the lepers, cast out devils. Provide neither silver or nor gold, nor brass in your purses.[96] He then threw away his staff, purse and shoes, and made these actions the rule of his life, preaching repentance and adopting a vow of poverty."[97]

Born in Avila, Spain on March 28, 1515, St. Teresa was the daughter of a Toledo merchant and his second wife, who died when St. Teresa was fifteen.[98] At any early age, she was sent to the Augustinian nuns to be cared for, and after reading the letters of St. Jerome, she chose to enter religious life. In 1535, she joined the Carmelite Order.[99] She spent much of this time trying to learn and practice mental prayer where she tried to keep Jesus Christ with her.[100] In her writings she says that she uttered, "My imagination is so dull that I had no talent

---

[95] Ibid., 2.

[96] Ibid.

[97] Ibid., 3.

[98] St. Teresa of Avila, *Spanish Carmelite Nun and Mystic*, ed. Benedict Zimmerman, trans. David Lewis (Grand Rapids, MI: Christian Classics Ethereal Library, 1904), accessed March 27, 2013, http://www.ccel.org/ccel/teresa/life.iv.html?highlight=st,teresa,of,avila,spanish,carmelite,nun,and,mystic#highlight.

[99] Ibid.

[100] *The Catholic Encyclopedia*, "St. Teresa of Avila," accessed March 27, 2013, http://www.newadvent.org/cathen/14515b.htm.

for imagining or coming up with great theological thoughts."[101] She continued to pray this way for the next eighteen years, feeling that she was getting little result.[102] She also is said to have suffered from the same problem as St. Francis of Assisi; she was too charming.[103] Everyone liked her and she found it too easy to slip into a worldly life and ignore God.[104] While she was encouraged to have visitors to whom she could teach mental prayer, St. Teresa tended to get more involved in flattery, vanity and gossip than spiritual guidance, and these small sins kept her from God.[105]

One day she fell ill with malaria and had a seizure, and it took four days for her to awaken. Afterwards, she was paralyzed for three years and she was never completely well.[106] She also chose not to pray during this time, making up excuses and saying that, "she didn't deserve favors from God."

Finally in 1553, Teresa experienced a vision of Jesus that resulted in spiritual conversion and drastically changed her relationship to God. In Chapter IX of her autobiography, *"The Life of Teresa of Avila,"* she provides an account of the moment of her conversion when she writes:

---

[101] Ibid.

[102] Ibid.

[104] Ibid.

[105] Ibid.

[106] Ibid.

> My soul was now grown weary; and the miserable habits it had contracted would not suffer it to rest, though it was desirous of doing so. It came to pass one day, when I went into the oratory, that I saw a picture which they had put by there, and which had been procured for a certain feast observed in the house. It was a representation of Christ most grievously wounded; and so devotional, that the very sight of it, when I saw it, moved me—so well did it show forth that which He suffered for us. So keenly did I feel the evil return I had made for those wounds, that I thought my heart was breaking. I threw myself on the ground beside it, my tears flowing plenteously, and implored Him to strengthen me once for all, so that I might never offend Him anymore.[107]

In this text, St. Teresa outlines her frustration with her failure to live what she considered a life dedicated to God, and she details the experience that finally led her to a feeling of remorse at how she must have offended God. According to St. Teresa in the Catholic Encyclopedia, this spiritual encounter allowed for the initial spiritual "progress" that she had so desired. In her own words she wrote, "the Saint progressed rapidly in virtue following this experience and she soon began enjoying visions and ecstasies. Following the initial experience, St. Teresa frequently writes about what she calls repeated "ecstatic" experiences during which she came to focus more sharply on Christ's passion.[108] She says that God gave her spiritual insights; prayers of quiet where God's presence overwhelmed her senses, raptures where God overcame her with glorious foolishness, and

---

[107] St. Teresa of Avila, *The Life of St. Teresa of Jesus, of the Order of Our Lady of Carmel,* ed. Benedict Zimmerman, trans. David Lewis (Grand Rapids, MI: Christian Classics Ethereal Library, 1904), accessed March 27, 2013, http://www.ccel.org/ccel/teresa/life.pdf.

[108] Ibid.

prayers of union where she felt God melt her soul away.[109] Sometimes her whole body was raised from the ground. These private experiences led her to believe that she was called to reform a spiritually decaying order with no other means than spiritual insight and fortitude.[110] She focused on reforming her order and mastering herself and her adherence to the rule.[111]

From 1560 until her death, she worked to establish the "shoeless Carmelites," an order of nuns who sought to fulfill the primary command to love God and neighbor.[112] They focused on achieving these lofty goals by leaving the world and remaining within the protective walls of the monastery, minimizing distractions and embracing silence that allowed space for contemplation and prayer.[113] She left to posterity many new convents and a significant number of written works including *The Way of Perfection, The Interior Castle, The Life of Teresa of Avila and The Meditations on the Canticle.*

The benefits to society of the life of St. Teresa were only possible because she, like many others, chose to believe and embrace a spiritual encounter leading

---

[109] St. Teresa of Avila, "The Life of St. Teresa of Jesus, of the Order of Our Lady of Carmel," Christian Classics Ethereal Library, accessed April 13, 2013, http://www.ccel.org/ccel/teresa/life.html.

[110] Terrance G.S.J. Walsh, "Writing Anxiety in Teresa's Interior Castle," *Theological Studies* 56, no. 2 (1995): 251-275.

[111] Ibid.

[112] "History and Goals of Carmel," Carmelite Monastery of the Sacred Hearts, accessed date, April 13, 2013, http://www.sistersofcarmel.org/history.htm.

[113] Ibid.

to a spiritual conversion that propelled her to use the God-given gifts, talents and abilities God had imbued within her. Many individuals, both historic and current day, testify that they have been changed, redirected and found their purpose in life simply because they chose to accept and exercise their God-given gifts, talent and abilities once they were revealed through a Holy Spirit rendering. Then as now, these experiences not only put individuals on the proper course for their lives as pre-ordained by God, but provide them with a more focused dedication to God and His church, a clearer understanding of who they are in Christ, access to both increased ability and spiritual authority, and the peace of knowing that they are doing exactly what God has requested of them. How powerful and effective could those who call themselves Christians be if they chose to follow the path of those mentioned above? What would happen if they truly sought God and because of that seeking, they had an encounter with the Holy Spirit that awakened their God-given gifts, talents and abilities and strengthened their commitment to both church and God? What power lies dormant that has not yet been fully investigated?

C. **Theological Foundation**

The theological reflection centered on the Doctrine of the Trinity, specifically the Holy Spirit, to fully examine the source of spiritual gifts. Secondly, this doctrine was used as a basis to explore how gifts, talents and abilities are made to operate within an individual. Additionally, the research explored scriptural references related to the God-given gifts, talents and abilities, mentoring and individual purpose.

Over the last fifty years, research notates a steep decline in worship attendance and church membership. The decline, especially within the 18-30 year-old age group, threatens to weaken the very core of church growth – continued membership through support and participation by the sons, daughters, nieces, nephews and grandchildren of elderly members. Churches must respond to this downturn aggressively and effectively if they are to survive. Report after report has shown that local congregations and entire denominations in North America and Western Europe are now in a statistical tailspin according to Jason Vickers in Minding the Good Ground: A Theology for Church Renewal. Statistics reported by local churches to the General Council of Finance and Administration of the United Methodist Church demonstrates that professions of faith membership in 2010 were down 1.4% over 2009, and average worship attendance was down 2.3% within that same time period. Also in 2009, membership decreased by 1.2% and attendance by 1.9%.

A five-year project headed by Barna Group president David Kinnaman, explored the opportunities and challenges of faith development among teens and young adults. The findings of the research are included in a book by Kinnaman titled, *"You Lost Me: Why Young Christians are Leaving Church and Rethinking Church."* The project was comprised of eight national studies that included interviews with teenagers, young adults, parents, youth pastors, and senior pastors. The study of young adults focused on those who were regular churchgoers to a Christian church during their teen years and explored their reasons for disconnection from church life after the ages of fifteen. Reason number two of the research suggests that young people are looking for a stronger spiritual experience in church. Both teens and "twenty-somethings" said that the experience of Christianity is shallow.[114] They described something lacking in their church experience. Thirty-one percent said that, "church is boring." Twenty-four percent said that "faith is not relevant to my career or interests or that the Bible is not taught clearly or often enough (23%). Twenty percent of these young adults who attended church as a teenager and then stopped said, "God seems missing from my experience of church.[115]"

Multitudes are dropping out of the church and many churches are dumbfounded for what to do. Most of these losses in numbers are occurring at the emerging adult level; a term coined by research professor Jeffrey J. Arnett in 2000 to describe individuals who are still transitioning from adolescence to adulthood. Many churches are at a lost for what to do. Some churches have offered more progressive church participation options like texting, tweeting and blogging while

---

[114] "General Council on Finance and Administration," *The United Methodist Church*, accessed November 2013, http://www.gcfa.org/data-services.

[115] Ibid.

in church and during the sermon. Others have upgraded their music ministries, offering a more contemporary repertoire.

Those approaches, according to author and pastor Dennis McCallum do not address the reasons for the decline, specifically among young adults. "Most churches have little or nothing going on with college students – the most promising age range for raising up workers who serve God long-term. I think it goes to show that churches are more interested in adults who pay the bills than in raising up workers.[116] If that is indeed the case, is there a remedy that can help churches to serve and address the needs of older adults and young adults at the same time? What if the solution simply lay in the obvious: helping individuals identify a godly call or spiritual gift, which would eventually propel them to fulfill their ordained spiritual purposes? The Doctrine of the Trinity, when taught as sound doctrine, could ultimately serve this purpose by developing Christians with long-term commitment to perform the work that they have been spiritually gifted to perform, while propelling them to a higher dedication to both God and the church.

Doctrine of the Trinity

The Doctrine of the Trinity is thought by some to be one of the most difficult aspects of Christianity to understand. However, Dr. Peter Bellini,

---

[116] Dennis McCallum, *Members of One Another: How to Build a Biblical Ethos into your Church* (Houston, TX: New Paradigm Publishing, 2010), 297.

Assistant Professor in the Practice of Global Christianity at United Theological Seminary who teaches and researches Trinitarian Mission Theology and Theosis, says the Trinity is not a riddle that we cannot understand nor is it unclear math. According to Dr. Bellini, "The Trinity is the basic grammar and logic of our theology and practice. Three persons are interrelated in a community of holy love, in one divine essence that births and grows all that we are and will be." The doctrine itself is foundational to the Christian faith, and is crucial for properly understanding what God is like, how God relates to individuals, and how individuals should relate to God.[117] Very little time, however, seems to be allocated to understanding the significance of this doctrine. In many instances, the mere thought of one God spoken of as a "triune God" can yield complete confusion and cause individuals to ignore this very important Christian doctrine. This lack of clarity during many people's initial introduction to Christianity possibly results in even more confusion about how the three different roles interrelate to each other. What is the relationship between God the Father, God the Son and God the Holy Spirit? How does this peculiar relationship affect individuals and what is the role that each of these serves in individual lives and their Christian journeys? Can this "Trinity" configuration offer guidance and input toward fulfillment of purpose? Most Christians, whether they have been

---

[117] Matt Perman, "What is the Doctrine of the Trinity," *Desiring God,* accessed January 23, 2006, http:www.desiringgod.org/resource-library/articles/what-is-the-doctrine-of-the-Trinity.

Christians for many years or recently joined the church, are oblivious to the power contained within this doctrine and how it can serve to prepare and propel them to fulfillment of their God-given call and purpose.

While the questions are many, the doctrine has the capacity to provide sustained direction and guidance to the practicing Christian. The Trinity itself offers a glimpse into the essence and operation of God, and outlines the connection between divine and human interaction. For those who take time to study and live by it, the Doctrine of the Trinity can offer the ability to understand the godly source that created them, the example set forth by Jesus that will mature and prepare them for service, and the spiritual connection and guidance that will move them to ultimately walk in their preordained godly call or spiritual gift. Simply put, the Trinity provides an understanding of God as the Creator of the vessel designed for a specific purpose, Jesus as the example of how our lives should be lived in order to faithfully live out this purpose, and the Holy Spirit as the enabler and igniter or this call or gifts, and the means by which we are perfected and gain the spiritual acumen necessary to bring the task to completion and finally reconcile with God. The doctrine can provide the basis for prolonged and practical application of godly principles that strengthen one's connection to the church.

Historical Foundations for the Doctrine of the Trinity

The Doctrine of the Trinity and its terminology are credited to Tertullian, a theologian who was the son of a Roman centurion from North Africa. Tertullian, born around 160 AD, converted to Christianity in 197 A.D., after receiving an education in literature and theology. He was a staunch defender of the Catholic faith, and in so doing he invented much of the Trinitarian terminology.[118] It is in Tertullian's writings that we first find the Latin word *"Trinity"* to describe the relationship between the Father, Son, and Holy Spirit, whom he taught were "one God in three persons." He further explained that the words described God the Father, the Son and the Holy Spirit as one in "essence, not one in Person."[119] Based on his theological concepts, God is one, but cannot be regarded as someone or something that is isolated from the created order. While the three persons of the Trinity are distinct, they are not divided. Matt Perman, senior director of strategy at DesiringGod in Minneapolis, Minnesota simplifies this idea by outlining what he believes to be three crucial truths related to the Trinity: (1) The Father, the Son and Holy Spirit are distinct Persons, (2) each person is fully God, (3) there is only one God. Perman goes further to say that each has a distinct center of consciousness, and while there is close unity

---

[118] Allan D. Menzies, "Latin Christianity, Its Founder, Tertullian," *The Writings of the Fathers Down to AD 325*, vol. 3, accessed November 10, 2013, http://www.ccel.org/ccel/schaff/anf03.toc.html#P334_131093.

[119] Ibid.

between them all, each is distinct from the other. They are different persons, not three different ways of looking at God and "the Father is not the Son, the Son is not the Holy Spirit, and the Holy Spirit is not the Father."[120]

Christian theology states that each person of the Trinity is fully God and combined, they operate in a distinct yet coordinated manner. The only way to truly grasp the concept is to admit that it may be beyond the limits of rational reasoning. In the Zondervan Pictorial Bible Dictionary Merrill C. Tenney states that, "It is important to realize that the doctrine of the Trinity has not been given to the Church by speculative thought. It is not an *a priori* concept, nor in any sense derived from pure reason. This doctrine has come from the data of historical revelation. In the process of history God has revealed Himself as one God, subsisting in three Persons."[121]

One interesting evaluative approach to the overarching demonstrative meaning of the Trinity has arisen throughout pastoral and theological society. Douglas Miller, for example, pastor of Community Alliance Church, sees the Trinity as ultimately important because it clearly indicates that God is a God of community. "It is about three persons of the Trinity who freely share one purpose of love for us. Further, it is about how all people are welcomed into God's community, and it is about a vision for human society where people freely co-

---

[120] Ibid.

[121] Merrill C. Tenney, *The Zondervan Pictorial Bible Dictionary* (Grand Rapids, MI: Zondervan Publishing House, 1967), 871.

operate with each other." This concept truly makes sense when one looks at the roles of each element of the Trinity.

Graham Tomlin of St. Paul Theological Centre agrees and adds that the Trinity is a call for people to invest in relationships. In excerpts of a speech presented by Tomlin at Holy Trinity Brompton, he states the Father, the Son and the Holy Spirit were "bound together in a perfect unity of love, before the creation of the world, and that fact places relationships and love at the heart of the Universe." "Long before he had laid down earth's foundation, he had us in mind and settled upon us as the focus of his love to be made whole and holy by his love." Tomlin adds that, "the Doctrine of the Trinity tells us that relationships are far more important than our careers, our holidays and our salaries. We cannot live in this life on our own because we are made for relationship. We are made in the image of God. A God who is Trinity. And because of that, we need to invest in relationships." Augustine adds to that discussion of relationship when he says, "He alone could say it who knew what it was to have God dwelling within him. God offers us a short route to the possession of himself. The Holy Spirit makes us dwell in God and God in us." That too, is indicative of the element of relationship and community prescribed by the Trinity.

Who is God the Father and what is God's role in a person's life? Who is Jesus Christ and how does the existence of Christ affect the Christian journey? What is the purpose and role of the Holy Spirit? Understanding the Trinity is difficult, but working to obtain clear perspective on the purpose and functioning of each "person" within the Trinity can bring clarity and purpose to individual lives. While we know God to be the infinite Creator, understanding the roles of Jesus Christ and the Holy Spirit can potentially provide more complication. In its simplest explanation based on biblical scripture, God is the Creator of life. God existed before time and called everything and everyone into being. Jesus Christ, who is said to have taken the form of man and come to earth, is the example. It is through Christ that one understands the road to salvation and the requirements and process of sanctification. Finally, the Holy Spirit is the enabler. It resides inside of individuals and guides them toward God, sanctification and life purpose. It is the giver and sustainer of all life, "the ongoing creator of all creatures and especially the animator of human beings."[122] Together these three "persons" serve to help individuals activate, navigate and sustain the Christian faith.

God the Father

Who indeed is God? We are often told that God is the Creator of the Universe. God is the supreme ruler over heaven and earth. It is to God that individuals must be reconciled with and God the Father is an essential part of the salvation process. God created both heaven and earth. In Judaism, God is described as Father because God is labeled with names including Creator, Life-

---

[122] A. C. Myers, *The Eerdmans Bible Dictionary* (Grand Rapids, MI: Eerdmans, 1987), 496-499.

Giver and Protector. Repentance is toward God and it is God who initiated the salvation process. God is the One who calls us out of this world.[123] Theologian Karl Barth believed that God was supreme and preeminent. He believed God to be so immense and powerful, that modern man could not fathom his power. "The power of God can be detected neither in the world of nature nor in the souls of men. It must not be confounded with any high, exalted, force known or unknown."[124] Alister E. McGrath in *"Christian Theology: An Introduction,"* also believes that an understanding of God in totality is virtually impossible. "The fundamental problem here is the inability of human language to do justice to the transcendent. Human language finds itself pressed to its limits when trying to depict and describe the divine."[125] So while individuals may never hope to grasp an understanding of God in totality, there is a clear understanding that God is the Creator and that everything was created by God for God's purpose, including people. That in itself provides a place to begin.

---

[123] Michael Bradley, "Seeking After the Knowledge of God," *PrayWay Global Prayer Community, 2005, a*ccessed November 12, 2013, http://www.prayway.com/articles/Seeking_After_the_Kn.htm.

[124] Karl Barth, *The Epistle of the Romans,* trans. Edwyn C. Hoskyns (London, England: Oxford University Press, 1933).

[125] Alister E. McGrath, *Christian Theology: An Introduction* (Kings College, NJ: John Wiley and Sons, Ltd., 2011), 234.

God the Son

The second person of the Trinity is Jesus Christ. Christ, simply put, is said to have provided a way to salvation and reconciliation with God. This salvation is grounded in the life, death and resurrection of Christ and Christ also serves to set an example of how to live. McGrath states that the Christian approach to salvation is distinct in two areas. "In the first place, salvation is understood to be grounded in the life, death, and resurrection of Jesus Christ; in the second, the specific shape of salvation within the Christian tradition is itself formed by Christ."[126] In other words, not only is salvation grounded in the life, death and resurrection of Christ, but that same journey ultimately outlines the course of action necessary to achieve oneness with God. McGrath also states that Christianity holds that salvation is only possible due to the journey of Jesus Christ.

More recent theological literature, however, challenges that notion and suggests that the question is whether Jesus Christ simply made public professions related to an unchangeable situation or actually established a new situation? In the Doctrine of Reconciliation, German theologian Martin Kahler moves the discussion to an ultimate question of whether the life of Jesus was merely illustrative or did it instigate something new. Did Jesus Christ merely demonstrate the saving will of God by going to the Cross or did going to the Cross originate

---

[126] Ibid., 316.

and make salvation possible for Christians? Possibly Jesus Christ came to reveal the saving nature of God, not establish that saving nature.[127]

Regardless of the conclusion, it is clear that the journey of Jesus Christ goes beyond the elements of salvation usually taught to Believers. Further exploration of that journey indicates that it also points at the way to salvation by demonstrating a model of Christian life. Jesus was sent to earth not only to "demonstrate God's love for us" as stated by Augustine, but also to "illuminate the world by his wisdom, and excite it to love of God," according to the theologian Peter Abelard.[128] It is evident that the journey of Jesus served a dual purpose that may not always be clearly explained. Jesus not only came to offer salvation in the afterlife, but also to offer life more abundantly to individuals even while they yet abide in the world. This became evident within the writings of theologian John B. Cobb in, *"Christ in a Pluralistic Age."* "I interpreted Jesus' message as one that disrupted the simple continuity of the hearers with the past in such a way as to open them to God's present gift of new possibility. I understood the new not as displacing the past or discontinuous with it, but rather as creatively transforming it. I proposed that Jesus' life and death generated a field of force and that to enter that field is to be opened to creative transformation."[129] Christology

---

[127] Alister E. McGrath, *Christian Theology: An Introduction*, 317.

[128] McGrath, 332.

[129] John Cobb, *Christ in a Pluralist Age,* 9.

indeed provides individuals with a literal road map to a reconnection with God in both the here and now and the future, and it does so through creative transformation of one's spiritual reality and spiritual relationship with God.

God the Holy Spirit

While it did indeed play a role in the early formation of Christianity, the early church had a challenging time understanding the concept of the Holy Spirit. According to McGrath, "the early church found itself puzzled by the Spirit and unable to make much in the way of theological sense of this area of the doctrine of God."[130] McGrath goes on to say that while there were those who focused on the activity of the Holy Spirit during this time like Montanus, a religious leader of the *illuminati,* there was a relative absence of discussion related to the role of the Holy Spirit during the first three centuries of the church. Therefore, the full divinity of the Spirit took place at a relatively late stage. The sequence of those stages included the recognition of the full divinity of Jesus Christ, the recognition of the full divinity of the Spirit and the formulation of the Doctrine of the Trinity, embedding and clarifying these central insights and determining their mutual relationship.[131] One of the most significant contributors to the development of the theology of the Holy Spirit, according to McGrath, was Augustine. He regarded

---

[130] Ibid., 228.

[131] Ibid., 230.

the Holy Spirit as the unifying bond between the Father and the Son, and between God and believers. Augustine believed that the Holy Spirit forged bonds of unity between believers, upon which the unity of the church ultimately depended.[132]

The Holy Spirit empowers individuals for service, according to The Eerdmans Bible Dictionary. "The work of the Spirit focuses on equipping and energizing various individuals for special service or tasks. It empowers artisans like Bezalel for the building of the tabernacle in Exodus 31:3; 35:31. Most often the Spirit is said to prepare and endow individuals for leadership; filling Joshua with the spirit of wisdom, preparing judges for Israel, giving Sampson extraordinary strength and power, and guiding kings. [133]

Christian tradition generally lists the work of the Holy Spirit as focused in three broad areas including revelation, salvation, and the Christian life. The task of the Holy Spirit is to lead into God's truth and within that truth, make God known to humanity. The Spirit is also said to be involved with human response to that revelation, essentially leading to faith. It serves to sanctify the human spirit, making humanity more like God. Finally, the Spirit energizes the Christian life. In addition, Christian theology often adds that the Holy Spirit serves to make God real during personal and corporate worship and devotion, as well as shapes and

---

[132] Ibid., 231.

[133] A. C. Myers, *The Eerdmans Bible Dictionary* (Grand Rapids, MI: Eerdmans, 1987), 496-499.

sustains the Christian community, fostering its witness to the world.[134] Pauline Theology dictates the purposes of the Holy Spirit. Paul believed that the Holy Spirit indwells in an individual to: enable believers to live a righteous and faithful life by directing them to obedience; provide the stamp of God's ownership that then bears witness with an individual's own spirit; allow for miracles, signs and wonders to occur; activate, pour out and perfect spiritual gifts and talents in an individual for the purpose of service to God.[135] Further, Pauline Theory states that the Holy Spirit has been conferred on all Believers in Christ, and serves to help with obedience to the law, as prophesied by Ezekiel.[136] Regardless of which description of the work of the Holy Spirit is chosen, it is clear that it plays an integral role in the spiritual development of Christians and that it can seemingly be used to increase one's connection to God and to instruct and guide individuals in the work that God has planned for them to complete.

When one takes into consideration the cumulative nature of the Trinity and the various roles played by each person of the Trinity, it cannot help but to become clear that there is great spiritual importance and benefit to teaching and implementing the principles associated with this doctrine. When viewed in

---

[134] John Cobb, *Christ in a Pluralist Age*, 232.

[135] Barry D. Smith, "The Holy Spirit in Pauline Theology," Atlanta Baptist University, March 27, 2006, accessed April 10, 2013, http://www.freerepublic.com/focus/f-religion/1614888/posts.

[136] Ibid.

concert with the obvious reduction in numbers of young adults and others attending or joining church, the empowering and spiritual pull of the Doctrine of the Trinity would seem to offer a viable anecdote to the problem. An understanding that God the Creator places gifts and talents within individuals for a purpose; that Jesus Christ demonstrates how to live a holy life in preparation for using those gifts and talents; and the Holy Spirit calls forth and perfects those gifts and talents through spiritual relationship with and preparation from God, could only serve to interest and excite individuals about the possibility of making a difference in life. If more time was allotted to teaching church members and potential church members the relevance of the Doctrine of the Trinity and how it plays out in the life of a Christian, enabling and sustaining spiritual connection to God and discovery of God-given gifts and talents, possibly more young adults would become engaged and involved in church.

If indeed the Doctrine of the Trinity is one of the most important and substantive elements of the Christian faith, one can easily anticipate that any disregard or absence of its presence within the church would result in declining numbers, challenges to the Christian faith, weakened spiritual acumen, and a host of other ills. Possibly a regeneration and clear explanation of the principles associated with this Doctrine: revelation of God's will for an individual's life, salvation and justification, spiritual gifts, and spiritual guidance; could help to personalize the Christian experience for individuals and propel them to eagerly and with commitment, live out their faith in both a spiritual and social context. The Doctrine of the Trinity, especially the Holy Spirit teachings, could ultimately be the balm that heals, restores and reignites Christianity and helps individuals to discover and ignite their godly calls or spiritual gifts and commit to both church and God.

D. Theoretical Foundation

Data was compiled based on an exploration of research on church attendance, participation and membership for the study age group, belief in God and understanding of the elements of Godly relationship and purpose. Additionally, "The Seven Vectors of Arthur E. Chickering's *Theory of Identity Development in Young Adults,*" was used as the primary theoretical foundation, complimented by ministry models applied by Agape Time Ministries, Inc. of St. Louis, MO.

Practical and appropriate methodologies timed with applicable developmental theories concerning emerging adults, can provide a successful convergence that can ultimately increase commitment to both church and God among this population. In essence, the ages of eighteen through thirty can prove to be a particularly opportune period to develop long-term habits in emerging adults. Many more young adults than in the past are choosing to pursue their education over a lengthier time period. They change majors while exploring careers, take courses while working full-time and taking their time finishing college. In addition, many of these individuals are constructing an identity; portions of which will remain with them for the rest of their lives. They are weighing possibilities, evaluating choices, and in general, working through life challenges, clearly open to acquiring the skills necessary to achieve in life and to successfully work through these challenges. For that reason, implementing a research project such as this during this time, that implements Holy Spirit gift identification, undergirded by the appropriate mentoring and leadership teaching, can prove invaluable to reaching the goal of commitment to church and God among this population.

Holy Spirit Gift Identification

The formal basis for the entire research project is the identification and activation of Holy Spirit gifts in each of the survey participants. Identifying these gifts, many of which are outlined in First Corinthians and Ephesians 4:11, provides an impetus for participants to acquire both the confidence and curiosity to move forward with support provided through the other elements of the research project.

Developmental Theories

Experts in the field of human development agree that adults within this age range are focused on exploring attitudes, values and life possibilities. This is a time during which these young adults engage in groundbreaking exploration, advancing in formation of their identities. Attitudes and values broaden, and a stronger interest is expressed in philosophical, historical and political issues. Ideally, these young adults are more open to connecting with God and the church than at any other time in their lives.

Renowned developmental psychologist and psychoanalyst Erik Erickson believes that these young adults are very confused about their identity, and struggle with what Erickson terms, "individual identity versus identity confusion."[137] They are relating to other human beings at a deep, personal level and are learning to give and share without asking what will be returned.[138] Personal identities are being developed, according to Erickson, and they are asking questions such as, "What is the meaning of my life?" "Who am I?" and "Where am I going in life?"[139] But, these questions make this the perfect time to present fresh ideas for consideration and exploration. If presented in a way that is personal and relatable, and that helps them to identify why they were created and what they were created for, ideas related to long term commitment to church and God can ultimately be sustained within them.

---

[137] Kendra Cherry, "Identity Versus Confusion: Stage Six of Psychosocial Development," About Psychology, accessed January 15, 2014, http://psychology.about.com/od/psychosocialtheories/a/intimacy-versus-isolation.htm.

[138] Ibid.

[139] Ibid.

While Erickson's work strongly informed the research, it is the work of Arthur Chickering, a leading researcher in student development that complemented the research project. Chickering's Seven Vectors of Identity Development provided a clear developmental path in emerging adults that yielded varied opportunities to implement the research. Those vectors of identity development included: Developing Competence, Managing Emotions, Moving through Autonomy toward Interdependence, Developing Mature Interpersonal relationships, Establishing Identity, Developing Purpose and Developing Integrity. The research model focused more specifically on applying opportunities within the various sectors of the model.

Developing Competence

Three developing competencies during college are intellectual, physical and manual skills, and interpersonal. Intellectual competence allows individuals to learn to use their mind by mastering content, becoming more intellectually sophisticated, and building a repertoire of skills to help one comprehend, analyze, and synthesize. It also includes developing new frames of reference that examine more points of view and help an individual develop a sense of personal observations and experiences. Physical and manual competence focuses on designing and making tangible products, and gaining strength, fitness, and self-discipline. Interpersonal competence involves not only the skills of listening, cooperating, and communicating effectively, but also the more complex abilities to tune in to another person and respond appropriately, to align personal agendas with the goals of the group, and to choose from a variety of strategies to help a relationship flourish or a group function. In this sector, a student's overall sense of competence increases as they learn to trust their abilities, receive accurate feedback from others, and integrate their skills into a stable self-assurance. The researcher's model offered opportunities to perfect each of these elements through small group discussion, leadership instruction and teaching opportunities, evangelism, prayer and meditation and biblical studies.

Managing Emotions

This sector focuses on an individual's ability to learn to manage emotions that could potentially derail the educational process if they become excessive or overwhelming. These emotions need good management, and they should be allowed to move the student into an awareness and acknowledgement. Positive development occurs as students learn appropriate channels for releasing irritations before they explode, dealing with fears before they immobilize, and healing emotional wounds before they infect other relationships.

The researcher's model is founded on Christian principles that teach individuals to live by spiritual laws and guidance, and to manage and bring emotional responses under the subjugation of the Holy Spirit. This stage could also help individuals transcend the boundaries of self, and derive new identities by bonding with another, or to feel part of a larger whole. The researcher's model allowed for both ample bonding with peers and identification as part of a larger effort.

Establishing identity

Identity development involves comfort with body and appearance, comfort with gender and sexual orientation, sense of self in a social, historical, and cultural context, clarification of self-concept through roles and life-style, sense of self in response to feedback from valued others, self-acceptance and self-esteem, and personal stability and integration. A solid sense of self can emerge at this point and elements of the proposed research will help to create that by identifying individual spiritual gifts and talents, and providing avenues for expression of personal views, comments on biblical and leadership concepts and the presentation of self-designed teaching opportunities. The model should help to bring clarity of identity at this critical stage.

Developing Purpose

Developing a sense of purpose echoes the primary focus of the researcher's model. At this stage of development, emerging adults may have the energy, but no destination or clarity around who they want to become. The research model is designed to help emerging adults increase their ability to understand their God-given purposes, and bring clarity to who they are. They are led to clarify goals, make plans and commit to further developing their Holy Spirit gifts and assignments because they more clearly understand who they are and what they are called to become through small group discussions, teaching and learning opportunities and gift activation and intentional use exercises. They are given the opportunity to acquire a more solid understanding of how their chosen vocational plans and aspirations, personal interests, and interpersonal and family commitments, all tie in to who they are called by God to become.

These vectors provide clear opportunities for the research model to capitalize on the various developmental stages of the participants. When coupled with and complemented by appropriate mentoring and leadership training, they can help to birth a desire to commit to church and God that will propel individuals throughout their lives.

Chapter 3

Methodology

A. <u>Spiritual Gift Identification and Activation</u>

As stated earlier, spiritual gift identification is the primary focus of the research and methodology. This is accomplished through prayer, surveys, one-on-one discussions, observation and individual study and prayer. Research participants complete several surveys throughout the course of the research project, at least two designed to help identify their spiritual gifting. Observable interactions, written work and personal conversations help to confirm the survey results. Participants are then allowed to research the particular area of their gifting, in preparation for opportunities to actually ignite and use those gifts. This is the primary element in the process and the development vectors as outlined by Chickering that will serve as a means to determine the most opportune times to teach the participants in this area.

B. <u>Mentoring</u>

"Mentoring relationships, in which a more experienced individual works to advance the personal and professional growth of a less experienced protégé, have witnessed a noteworthy increase in use as a mechanism for leadership development."[140] While this is true, mentors must employ effective strategies for mentoring emerging adults if young adults are to be reached. The researcher examined various mentor relationships throughout the Bible, ultimately presenting the relationship between Paul and Timothy as an example of successful strategies that lead an individual to long-term commitment to both church and God. Paul, as the loving mentor to Timothy, provides for an excellent discourse on what it actually means to be an effective mentor, specifically as it relates to this research project. Additionally, the researcher examined several church models, eventually focusing on a model that is applied at Agape Time Ministries, Inc. in St. Louis, MO., as one that most closely resembles that which is necessary to accomplish the desired outcome of the research.

To begin with, mentors are those who offer support, guidance and wisdom, preferably in a healthy environment, designed and developed for individual growth. It is imperative that they allow individuals opportunities to expand and grow and to ask questions, and yet allow them to formulate their own answers, and to test new ideas and theories that may not immediately line up with the agenda of the mentor, in this case those ideas related to the church or the Bible. While it is understood that all mentors must model and exemplify that which they are attempting to instill, it also is very necessary that mentors focus on equipping,

---

[140] John Sosik, Doris Lee, and Edward Bouquillon, "Context and Mentoring: Examining Formal and Informal Relationships in High Tech Firms and K-12 Schools. *"Journal of Leadership and Organizational Studies"* 12 (2005) 94-109.

engaging, and empowering those same individuals. If these three elements are not present, the mentoring may prove not to be successful.

Equipping

The first necessity of any mentor is that they equip individuals. Mentors must ensure that those who are to be mentored by them have the items necessary for success in a particular area and that those items are presented in a manner that is conducive to learning. As it related to this research project, that means that mentors must be chosen who clearly understand what is needed to fully serve God and the church. For example, if an individual does not understand the concept of commitment and is not provided with clear explanations and demonstrations of what it looks like, how then can they be expected to be committed to anything, let alone those things that require constant reinforcement such as relationships to church and God. If mentoring is to prove beneficial to the mentee, the mentor and the overall organization that it will ultimately benefit must be employed in a strategic and encompassing manner that submerges individuals in the necessary elements.

Another element that must be in place is a strong example of some of the proposed research concepts already being implemented. Agape Time Ministries, Inc. City of Refuge, in St. Louis, Missouri served in this capacity. Agape Time, founded and led by pastors John and Pamela Dillon, was structured to "produce and promote God's leaders for service to His people, the body of Christ, through mentorship and fellowship."[141] Within the workbook that outlines the work of the ministry, the pastors focus on many applied methodologies, including one that focuses on prayer. They take young adults through a demonstrative process of prayer that uses visualization, such as settings in a large circle and the Mosaic Tabernacle placed on a table in the middle of that circle, designed to cause a more impactful and effective learning moment.[142] While this exercise demonstrates the modeling concept – prayer is led by one of the pastors – it also clearly equips participants for a life of prayer by emphasizing the ultimate importance of it, and demonstrating the means by which it proves to be most effective in an individual's life. The workbook also provides portions of the dialogue that accompanies this prayer teaching and demonstration, which occurs on Monday evenings each week. Clear explanation, a demonstration of what is expected and consistent reinforcement of the importance of what is being taught, will ensure that mentees are properly equipped to serve and understand the elements needed to succeed in that service.

The ministry also equips its participants by setting aside time for the leaders in training to speak individually with the pastors concerning life issues. "One on Ones allow us to evaluate the growth of the leader and to show them how

---

[141] Pamela K. Dillon, *Encounters with Leadership* (Bloomington, IN: WestBow Press, 2013) v.

[142] Ibid., 9.

amazingly God has brought them from one point to the next. In addition, the quality time of listening to the leader's heart about certain issues pertaining to their teammates or just life in general, is a very detoxifying and refreshing part of their development."[143]

Engaging

Any mentor must fully engage those they are charged to mentor so that individuals feel involved, and not simply experientially engaged through showing up, watching and listening. To engage can mean to become involved in or partake of, but synonyms for it indicate that it also can mean capture, arrest or attract. If mentors truly want to attract and retain the attention of those that they are instructing, they must implement methodology that emphasizes an engaging method of instruction. "Research has shown that quality teacher-student interactions far outweigh all other considerations to produce positive learning outcomes."[144] In general, people tend to feel more satisfied and achieve more when they can actively contribute to the process of learning, so mentoring should clearly be focused on engaging participants at every level along the way.

Agape Time indicates that it encourages its leaders in this area as well. Each Tuesday evening, those in training under the ministry are assigned to teach

---

[143] Ibid., 13.

[144] Robert F. Kenny and Jeffrey Wirth, "Implementing Participatory Construction Learning Experience Through Best Practices in Live Interactive Performance. *The Journal of Effective Teaching,* vol. 9, No. 1, 2009, 34-47.

classes. Many of these lessons focus on teaching "character" as a means to impart godly character among the group. "Each member is given a character trait such as longsuffering or loyalty. We also teach from John Maxwell's 21 Irrefutable Laws of Leadership," Pastor Pamela Dillon says in the training manual."[145] Within the manual, the leadership indicates that it believes that this methodology brings with it accountability, respect and healthy character, all necessary elements for those planning to serve God.

Empowering

Equipping and engaging individuals leads to empowerment of those individuals. Within the mentoring methodology of Agape Time opportunities are provided for mentees to practice their Holy Spirit-given gifts in a formal, but safe environment. On Expression Sundays, leaders are led to participate in a service similar to a traditional church worship service. For many, it is their debut of the gifts and talents that God has given to them.

While it is a controlled environment, outside guests are invited and encouraged to attend, so in all aspects it is a real life situation. "Expression Sunday helps the leader to become skilled in identifying different types of spiritual activity whether it is demonic hindrance or Holy Spirit led. It helps the leader to actively discern what they see in the spirit realm while at the same time,

---

[145] Pamela K. Dillon, *Encounters with Leadership*, 23.

performing their God-given talk or assignment for the day."[146] Empowerment in this way allows mentees to build confidence in their abilities, challenges them to commit to the process of discerning and fully using those abilities, and focuses them on perfecting and committing to a God that consistently increases and perfects those abilities. In addition, there is a realization of the spiritual power and authority that they possess, and recognition that there is responsibility that partners with it. They become personally affected and touched, and the commitment becomes strengthened.

C. Leadership Development and Training

Leadership training is the final element that should be added to the broad mix of components that will effectively cause commitment to church and God within emerging adult populations. This element of the instruction includes participation in various activities that teach biblical leadership principles, allowing research participants to become teachers themselves. Each is assigned three lessons to research and teach during the research period. Those lessons focus on biblical principles, concepts and character, and overall leadership principles. In addition, participants are asked to support the church by volunteering to help with at least two service opportunities each year, and help to plan and implement events that show others their connectedness to church and God.

---

[146] Ibid., 31.

Much of the training focuses on leadership principles, as outlined in Stephen Covey's *Seven Habits of Highly Effective People,* and John Maxwell's *The 21 Irrefutable Laws of Leadership.* These two books, coupled with the study of biblical leadership examples and opportunity to exercise and grow in the capacity for leadership, should successfully prepare these individuals to become leaders for God.

John Maxwell, pastor turned leadership guru, has sold more than 70 books and conducted 1,000s of speaking engagements related to leadership. His single focus throughout the years has been his desire to develop the leadership potential in other individuals and his pastoral background helps to inform this research project. The researcher's leadership model, based on some of the principles outlined in his work, does not focus on teaching people what you believe that they should know, but engaging them in learning about those things that will equip them to learn what they need to learn, and lead as they will need to lead. According to Maxwell, leadership indeed is influence and in order to prepare individuals to follow that which Jesus has requested in The Great Commission, Matthew 28:19-20, we must all learn to both teach and effectively lead.

Maxwell states that, "A leader is one who knows the way, goes the way, and shows the way.[147]" This is the prescription for a world often void of true

---

[147] John Maxwell, *The 21 Irrefutable Laws of Leadership* (Nashville, TN: Thomas Nelson Publishers, 2007), 15.

Christian leadership, and Maxwell's work can serve as a road map to fill that void. Those engaged in the project are led not only to learn successful leadership principle's supported by strong biblical examples and references, but also to teach these principles within a Christian context.

In addition to Maxwell's leadership principles, research study group participant's study biblical examples of leadership, such as Moses, Peter, Paul, Nehemiah, Joshua, Barnabas and Elijah. They are asked to closely examine the successes and failures of these leaders, and to track what made them effective at fulfilling their God-given purpose and using their spiritual gifts and talents.

Throughout the research project, several of the elements used within Agape Time's leadership mix also are applied, in conjunction with activities developed and designed by the researcher. Those included teaching participants to pray by using a leadership model designed by Agape Time, an opportunity to host and manage a group-sponsored healing service at the church, writing assignments that produced a book of essays for emerging youth, an opportunity to minister to others outside of the church during a "ministry field trip" and finally, the opportunity to create additional ministries for the church.

The church sorely needs to raise and develop young leaders who will commit to serving God and God's people, both inside and outside the confines of the church. Current models of leadership preparation or duplication seem to be accomplishing little; at least if one is to use the current exodus of emerging adults from the pews of churches as a foretelling. It is imperative that the church and those who serve God create leadership models that inspire commitment to both the church and God by young people who have the energy, the tools and the desire to serve in a long-term manner. The researcher believes that this model, based on research results, can help to accomplish that goal.

Chapter 4

Project Analysis, Methodology, Summary, Conclusions

The project of ministry presented within this document was developed to address the needs of declining church attendance and commitment to God among young adults; those aged eighteen to thirty who are experiencing life between adolescence and adulthood. The purpose of this study was to discover if teaching Holy Spirit gifts, as outlined in First Corinthians 12 and Ephesians 4:11-12, and providing the opportunity to practice using those gifts, coupled with strong mentorship and applicable leadership training, would increase commitment to church and God.

The research examined initial beliefs and attitudes about church, God and religion in general. Initial responses were noted and contained within an initial survey, which was then measured against additional surveys rendered at twelve months and two years. Comparison data was compiled that also took into account information from data related to participation and attendance, small group interaction and discussion, written essays, and response to mentoring and leadership training.

This research has proven to be both viable and applicable for addressing the problem area, based on this researcher's experiences with church and God as a young adult, the long-term research with a designated group of those within the target profile, as well as additional research, such as that offered in *Lost and*

Found: The Younger Unchurched and the Churches that Reach Them by Ed Stetzer, Richie Stanley and Jason Hayes. Young adults are searching for significance and they genuinely desire to know who they are and what they are becoming. They want to go in deep with God.[148] The context for the two-year study was Wellspring Church in Ferguson, Missouri, a United Methodist church launched on September 11, 2011. The researcher was part of the initial launch team, serving as both the church administrator and the college-age minister.

The study began in August 2012 and concluded in August 2014, though members of the group are still engaged today. Much of the analysis comes from a Pew Research telephone survey conducted Feb. 14-23, 2014 among a national sample of 1,821 adults, including an oversample of young adults ages 18 to 33. Interviews were conducted on landline telephones (481) and cell phones (1,340) under the direction of Princeton Survey Research Associates International. The margin of sampling error is plus or minus 2.6% for results based on the total sample at the 95% confidence level. Additional analysis is based on two Pew Research Center telephone surveys conducted Jan. 23-Feb. 9, 2014 and Feb. 12-26, 2014 among national samples of adults. For both surveys, interviews were conducted on landline telephones (1671/1671) and cell phones (1670/1667) under the direction of Abt SRBI. Each of the surveys has a margin of sampling error of

---

[148] "Millenials in Adulthood," Pew Research Center, accessed January 15, 2014, http://www.pewsocialtrends.org/2014/03/07/millennials-in-adulthood/.

plus or minus 2.0% for results based on the total sample at the 95% confidence level. The length of the study coincided with research by The Pew Research Center that indicates individuals in the age category, eighteen to thirty, possess low levels of social trust.[149] Therefore, time was needed to build trust. Ten individuals, five males and five females, began and completed the study.

Project Design

The project began with telephone calls to establish the relationships necessary to create an interest in participating in the project. Since there had been a high degree of engagement with young adults since 1988, there was a pool of potential participants available among those who had already established friendships, relationships and other relationships with the researcher. Contact cards were added as an additional means to reach out to potential research participants, and individuals were asked to call if they were interested in prayer and in discovering their God-given gifts. At that time, there was no clear mention of the Holy Spirit, because it may have been possible that many of them would not have understood that reference. The pool of participants was also selected based on them being either unchurched or having not attended church since childhood, as evidenced by initial discussions upon meeting the individuals.

Of the initial twenty-five telephone contacts, ten individuals were invited to participate, five females and five males of varied socio-economic status, to participate in the two-year process. The female study group participants consisted of one 25-year-old female, two 24-year-old females, one 21 year-old female, and one 20-year-old female. Male study group participants consisted of one 29-year-old male, one 25-year-old male, one 24-year-old male, one 23-year-old male, and one 22-year-old male.

Once selected, each participant was told that the process would help them to discover what they had been created for, provide them with information about their particular gift or talent, as well as give them the opportunity to exercise those spiritual gifts in a safe environment. In addition, they were told that they would also receive leadership development training and learn about God and the Bible.

The project was established to revolve around twice monthly meetings on Saturdays and some Sundays, for approximately a three-hour period, which included lunch. Content within these meetings focused primarily on providing intimate, small group discussion around relevant biblical topics, leadership development by applying biblical lessons and teaching from the book, *"The 21 Irrefutable Laws of Leadership: Follow Them and People Will Follow You,"* by John C. Maxwell, and examining Christian character development topics like love, obedience, humility and servant hood, Holy Spirit gift identification, activation and demonstration, and prayer.

While the researcher initially took the lead on many of these activities throughout the first year, by month fourteen, the researcher began to select individuals to lead prayer or close the meeting with prayer, usually without letting them know ahead of time. This was done as a means to build trust with the participants and to gauge progressive levels of trust as the group continued to meet.

For the initial year, these activities, excluding prayer, were led by the researcher or a professional associate selected to teach on a particular topic, but after that timeframe when trust was established, participants were provided with their own topics to teach, and were given opportunities to lead discussions and spiritual gift demonstrations.

Most of the work within the research project occurred during small group meetings; meetings that provided time for intimate instruction and discussion about biblical and societal leadership principles, prayer, scripture, spiritual gift identification, and personal challenges and issues, and questions. Meetings also provided opportunities to learn through gift demonstrations and sharing personal testimonies, spiritual victories and individual life challenges.

In addition to the small group meeting activities, throughout the two-year process, participants were invited to attend church events, strategic planning activities, church meetings, and other activities related to leadership development and biblical teaching. They were also exposed to events that allowed them to encounter individuals of the same age and background, who were involved with church and God in some way, in order to build affinity.

The underlying assumption was that commitment to both church and God for those in this age group is inextricably tied to an understanding of who they are, what they were created to do, and how this knowledge can inform and enlighten their everyday lives.

The ministry model design consisted of the primary elements including spiritual gift identification and implementation opportunities, leadership development instruction and mentoring. Primary spiritual gifts were identified for each participant through spiritual assessments and prayer, and each participant was afforded the opportunity to exercise those spiritual gifts and talents in small group meetings, during church events and while participating in church services.

The element of leadership development instruction included participation in various activities that taught both biblical and mainstream leadership principles, with a goal of developing both leaders and teachers. Participants were assigned three lessons to research and teach during the research period. In addition, participants were asked to support the church by volunteering to help with at least two service opportunities each year, and helping to plan and implement events that showed others their connectedness to church, God, and the community.

The mentoring aspect focused on the mentor serving as an experienced and trusted advisor seeking to offer support, guidance and wisdom. In this case, the researcher served as the primary mentor to the participants, offering spiritually and biblically based solutions to everyday problems, concerns or challenges. Participants received various forms of support including individual prayer, assistance with setting and maintaining goals, and help working through other personal challenges by applying leadership and biblical principles. In addition, they are assigned opportunities to mentor each other and others outside of the group, in order to become effective in the mentoring role.

Methodology

As defined in William R. Meyers, *"Research in Ministry: A Primer for the Doctor of Ministry,"* the proactive research methodology is conducted when the researcher intentionally engages in qualitative research, and is passionately involved with the practice being evaluated."[150] As the college-age minister overseeing the study group, the researcher chose to conduct a qualitative study that employed a proactive research methodology. The qualitative study method was selected to allow for documentation and research instrumentation that tracks and traces changes in behavior and beliefs measured through cognitive interviews, surveys, structured observation of small group discussions, participant essays, and

---

[150] William R. Meyers, *Research in Ministry: A Primer for the Doctor of Ministry Program* (New York, NY: Exploration Press, 2000), 29.

attendance and participation in Sunday worship, as well as study group and other church activities.

The researcher selected a qualitative study approach that utilized Ethnography, defined as, "a strategy of inquiry in which the researcher studies an intact social group in a natural setting over a prolonged period of time by collecting, primarily observational and interview data."[151] The researcher maintained direct interaction with the study group individuals, serving as mentor and observer, in both group settings and on an individual basis.

Research methodologies for the research included cognitive interviews and pre- and -post surveys to determine changes in awareness, perception and reasoning and changes in action and attitudes; structured observations during small group settings; attendance and participation tracking for Sunday worship, leadership training classes, and other church activities; and essays.

Hypothesis testing measured changes in thought and action, participation in leadership training and other leadership activities, acceptance of and operation in a Holy Spirit gift, and attitude changes about church and God.

Data-Analysis Process

The researcher played an active role as a participant who both observed and shared through table-fellowship, mentoring and theological instruction, personal and spiritual guidance. The process of data analysis involved observation

---

[151] John H. Creswell, *Research Design: Qualitative, Quantitative, and Mixed Methods Approaches* (Thousand Oaks, CA: SAGE Publications, 2009), 13.

during meetings and other activities, the close reading of surveys, written documentation from brief essays and in-session writing assignments, and one-on-one interviews. This allowed for the tracking of changes and emergent patterns.

As time went on, the establishment of trust, in the process, the mentor and their peers, was evident among members of the group. Additionally, the acceptance of spiritual gifting and church as part of their daily life and regime were emergent patterns as well. These ideas eventually became embedded in each member of the group. Peer influence definitely played a role within the group as participants began to remind one another to study, read the Bible or simply come to class. These (and other) indicators were consistently being observed by the researcher within the areas of the data collection process and data was analyzed by the use of both qualitative tools to measure subjective details and quantitative tools to measure increased commitment through participation. The following methods of data-analysis were implemented including observation, on site surveys, documents, interviews, validity, credibility, transferability, triangulation, dependability, and confirmability.

Observation

The researcher compiled field notes by conducting observations as both an observer, notating individual responses, thoughts and feelings, and a participant, teaching about Holy Spirit gifts, leadership and biblical scripture. This method of data collection encompasses collecting information by "seeing" and "listening."

[152] Meetings were held on the first and second Sundays of each month and the primary observation activities occurred during this timeframe. However, the researcher also observed participant activities during attendance at church, study group events, and church-sponsored events and activities.

On-site Surveys

Initial surveys were conducted during the group's first meeting to gauge individual familiarity and attitudes toward church attendance and membership, ideas about and understanding of Christianity and God, life challenges and specific questions that they wanted addressed, knowledge of God-based gifts and talents, and overall reason for joining the study group.

In August 2013, a one-year survey was conducted to gauge the length of participation in study group, what had been gained or learned during that participation, changes in ideas, beliefs and feelings, and suggested improvements or activities to be added to the study model.

Finally, the researcher administered a two-year survey in August 2014. That survey attempted to help the researcher understand what Jason Vickers outlines in his book, *Minding the Good Ground: A Theology for Church Renewal,* when he states, that there has been a "decline in worship attendance and church membership among this age group because they have lost their interest in

---

[152] John W. Creswell, *Research Design: Qualitative, Quantitative, and Mixed Methods Approaches* (Thousand Oaks, CA: SAGE Publications, 2009), 119.

attending church and participating in church-related activities."[153] Included were questions about the participant's initial choice to attend, why they continued attending, whether they now belonged to a church and why or why not, and attitudinal changes about church attendance and God. All surveys were conducted at the primary observation sight, Wellspring Church, and during the established meeting time frames on Sundays after church.

Documents

In April 2013, participants were asked to write brief essays outlining how they felt about the study group and why they believed it was important to them. In August 2013, they were asked to write essays related to topics including Going to Church, What God Feels Like, Saying "Yes" to God, and What Really Has Changed. These responses produced a work booklet for Emerging Adults, entitled *Why Yes to God: Essays on Life and God by Young Adults* and served as an excellent monitor for changes in attitudes, beliefs and actions of the participants. In addition the booklet, which includes reference scriptures and space for individual notes, also serves as a strong leadership development tool since the group photo was included on the booklet and many have since been asked about their participation in both the group and the writing of the booklet. In addition, the

---

[153] Jason E. Vickers, *Minding the Good Ground: A Theology for Church Renewal* (Waco, TX: Baylor University Press, 2011), 6.

researcher was able to track attendance and participation under this collection method.

Interviews

Throughout the two-year study, the researcher consistently scheduled what were labeled as "one-on-one" meetings with individual group participants. While there were frequently opportunities for ministry, mentoring and discussion over the telephone at any given interval, the researcher also scheduled times to meet with each one of the study group participants throughout the eighteen months of the study. Approximately twenty individual meetings were conducted, sometimes within the context of the study, but most often at restaurants, movies or other outings agreed to by the researcher and participant. These provided opportunities for private, in-depth discussions related to participant feelings, attitudes and observations.

The above survey instruments were selected because all were relatively inexpensive, allowed for immediate access to data by the researcher, and were convenient since they allowed the researcher to perform as both participant and observer. Specifically, observation allowed the researcher to take advantage of first-hand experience with the participants, and the researcher could record information as it happened. It also allowed for a certain amount of comfort to be present within the group since the researcher was already a trusted individual with group participants. Additionally, the researcher was afforded the opportunity to compile attendance and participation data, both to be used as a gauge of participant commitment and interest.

Surveys were easily established and allowed participants to privately express their ideas and attitudes, without fear of rejection or correction by the group or the researcher. They also allowed for a standardized form of questioning that made comparisons between various respondents more easily made. The researcher was afforded a window into the private thinking of the participants, and at the same time, the questions were general enough in nature to allow for some relational thought patterns.

Documents were critical to the study because they allowed participants to provide input using their own words and observations. These were easily administered during scheduled meeting times, did not require the researcher to transcribe any data, and allowed for more thoughtful reflection since the participants were given all of the time that they believed they needed to complete the essays. These documents also allowed the researcher to discover first-hand why they valued the group and what they believed was beneficial about the group. To combat the fear of not being able to express oneself in a grammatically correct or articulate manner, the researcher emphasized that group members should not focus on correct grammar and that the researcher would be available to speak with them about any challenges that they might have writing the material.

Finally, the face-to-face interviews were invaluable because participants were interviewed within an environment in which they could relax and be comfortable. No one was near to hear their comments and they were guaranteed anonymity by the researcher. Interviews were also effective data collection methods because those within this age group tend not to openly express all of their thoughts and concerns within a group setting. As developmental psychologist and psychoanalyst Erik Erickson states, this is a time when young adults are struggling with "individual identity versus identity confusion," and this could potentially cause them to be more hesitant to share untested perceptions and beliefs.[154] The researcher found that while participants actively engaged during group discussions, many more ideas and thoughts were shared during individual meetings. This type of collection method also provided the researcher with a measure of control over the questions and discussion.

Validity

It is understood that a valid qualitative research project will ensure that the tested outcomes are true and certain, and that the results are observable. Throughout the implementation of the project, the researcher worked to ensure credibility of the research, and did not over generalize the results. The researcher applied integrity in noting universal observations and conclusions, and while

---

[154] Kendra Cherry, "Identity Versus Confusion: Stage Six of Psychosocial Development," *About Psychology*, http://psychology.about.com/od/psychosocialtheories/a/intimacy-versus-isolation.htm.

transferability of the project may not be expansive due to the very specific context, project outcomes can be used to examine additional research in varying contexts. The researcher also noted and documented any changes that occurred during project implementation, and drew conclusions as to the overall impact of those changes, if any, to the stated outcome of the study. Timely and well-written documentation of observations as the project unfolded helped to confirm or contradict assumptions that the researcher outlined ahead of time.

Credibility

Selection of participants was non-random in that participants were of the same age bracket, from the same community, and all had a desire to know and understand their spiritual gifts. While not all of the participants had prior contact with the researcher before joining the study group, all had prior knowledge of the researcher either through earlier contact or through word-of mouth. The researcher participated in the selection process, but a context associate also confirmed selected participants. This decision helped to prevent personal bias by the researcher related to study group participation and the selection process.

All participants in the study group were straightforward and forthcoming with information and the researcher made sure not to ask leading questions or to state opinions as facts. Participants were informed that they should provide input based on their own thoughts, experiences and knowledge, and not based on what they thought they were expected to believe or think, especially as related to surveys being administered or the written input requested from them. Since the researcher was aware of playing the dual role of researcher and mentor to the group, it was repeatedly emphasized that survey group participants should answer exactly how they felt so as to inform both the researcher and the outcome of the study, and make it more valuable to serving other emerging adults. They were continuously encouraged to respond openly and honestly, and the researcher offered several opportunities for individual responses in which no name was recorded. Finally, questions and discussion content were designed to be probing and self-reflective so that participants would be required to take honest assessments of their thoughts, opinions and attitudes.

Transferability

Being aware of inherent assumptions at the start of a project can help safeguard the validity of a project's overall findings. Some of the assumptions the researcher brought to the start of the project were based on the researcher's experiences as an emerging adult. The researcher believed that in order to have a full and rewarding relationship with God, the Holy Spirit must be activated, as exampled in the following scriptures: Acts 2:4 where the Holy Spirit empowers people; Acts 1:16 where the Holy Spirit speaks and enables others to speak; and Acts 13:4 where the Holy Spirit sends individuals out in service to God. While the researcher had little knowledge of spiritual gifts as those mentioned in both the New and Old Testaments, the researcher believed that there was a power contained within the Holy Spirit that would allow individuals to do even greater works than those currently being performed. Throughout the Bible, evidence exists that individuals were consistently led away from their everyday lives to serve God in various capacities, directed by the Holy Spirit. The Holy Spirit led them to surrender themselves to God, sometimes alone and at others times through those chosen to provide prophetic leadership by igniting and initiating spiritual gifts and talents. Even Jesus, throughout the New Testament, led people to God through the Holy Spirit on the Day of Pentecost and through the individual work of the Disciples. After being accosted in one of these ways, individuals were led to dedicate themselves to the church and God. After reviewing the Biblical stories of individuals such as Jeremiah, Joel, David, Timothy, Titus, Paul and a host of others, the researcher strongly believed that individuals could be handpicked by God to complete a specific service, at a specific time, for a specific purpose by employing pre-ordained spiritual gifts. Paul substantiates the existence of these gifts and their initiation in individuals when he says in First Corinthians 2:12, "Now we have received, not the spirit of the world, but the spirit which is of God; that we might know the things that are freely given to us of God." He goes further to say that "there are diversities of gifts, but the same Spirit. There are differences of ministries, but the same Lord. And there are diversities of activities, but it is the same God who works all in all," (1 Cor. 12:4-7). Ephesians 4:11-13, also states that "And He Himself gave some to be apostles, some prophets, some evangelists, and some pastors and teachers, for the equipping of the saints for the work of ministry, for the edifying of the body of Christ."

The researcher always believed that if individuals could discover the fullness of the Holy Spirit, as highlighted in Pauline Theology, they could do immeasurable good and reside squarely within the will of God. This was the greatest assumption that was brought to the study group by the researcher. Based on that assumption, the researcher fully expected to see a change in church attendance and attitudes toward church and God, at the end of the study.

The researcher also assumed that a strong mentoring relationship, coupled with classroom instruction, would be needed to supplement the mere teaching of spiritual gifts, in order to initiate a stronger connection to church for those within the study group. The desire to commit to God and church, according to research on emerging adults and church affiliation and the researcher's experience, must be grounded in individuals who are committed to teaching, guiding and directing people through the learning process, as well as a curriculum that provides them with information and direction to maintain and grow those new spiritual connections.

Finally, the researcher believed that the study group would be strengthened if there were familiarity of the researcher by the group participants, primarily through prayer and spiritual guidance, as well as affinity within the group through prior relationships such as friendships and siblings.

Triangulation

Two methods of triangulation were utilized to help ensure project credibility. As a way to triangulate data two gift assessment surveys were used; Lifeway Christian Resources 80-question gifts survey and the Wagner-Modified Houts Questionnaire by the Charles E. Fuller Institute, a 125-question spiritual survey. Each study group participant completed one survey during the first quarter of the research and the other during month eighteen of the research. This helped the researcher assess and confirm spiritual gifts for each person within the study group.

The second method of triangulation involved the use of multiple qualitative instruments to track changes during the program. These included an initial survey completed during the first small group meeting, various essays and written materials completed by participants during the two-year study, mid-course surveying, and researcher observations and documentation during opening, mid-course and final quarter one-on-one meetings with study group participants.

Interpretation of the data was fairly straightforward, and the researcher employed the support of a context associate to confirm preliminary details. All tests and surveys were designed to show changes in attitude, thoughts and behaviors related to church attendance and participation, as well as consistency with Erickson's Model of human development in emerging adults. Additionally, survey answers sought to determine if participants have obtained any clarity on the most pressing questions during the life period, according to Erickson, including, "What is the meaning of my life?" "Who am I?" and "Where am I going in life?"[155]

Dependability

Initially the researcher was aware that mortality might be an issue. It was expected that some participants might cease to attend the study group due to a lack of desire to fully commit to the demands that accompanied the journey, or other life changes as indicative of the emerging adult period of life. The researcher, through relationship with various students as an adjunct instructor, was poised to meet these potential changes by being prepared for any mid-course-change corrections or creating additional testing methodology or mentoring activities in order to address these changes and safeguard the project.

There was no attrition within the initial study group of participants and participation was consistent and continuous by the ten participants. While some chose not to participate in all of the same voluntary and peripheral study group activities, there was a continued committed to the primary requirements of the project.

Confirmability

Throughout the process, the researcher documented observations with respect to negative or positive experiences by participants in the study group

---

[155] Ibid.

through one-on-one discussions, and shared the results of the overall program with those same participants in an attempt to confirm findings. In addition, small group discussion times were used to gain participant insight and to learn from them particular elements of the program that most resonated with them, and strengthened their desire to learn and work in their spiritual gifts. These findings were used to strengthen the program and to plan continued emerging adult ministry focused on this same research.

Project Timeline

The project timeline for the study was August 2012 through August 2014 and included the following implementation activities:

August 2012 – Initial contact and recruiting:

The researcher established the initial contacts through telephone prayer and mentoring. Initial participants were students in the researcher's college English courses, or were introduced to the group by a friend. From these groups, individuals were eventually selected to participate in the study project.

August 2012 – Initial College-Age Ministry meeting held at Wellspring Church:

An initial meeting was held at Wellspring Church in July. During this meeting, a small group discussion was facilitated, an initial survey was administered, and spiritual gift assessment questionnaires were completed.

October 2012 – December 2012:

Initial discussions of group goals, necessary commitment level, expectations, leadership principles, and results of initial gift assessment questionnaires occurred. Small group discussions continued, and clarity about spiritual gifts, including five-fold ministry gifts and others as defined in First Corinthians 12:7-11 and Ephesians 4:9-16 were discussed and explained. The group was introduced to the concept of sharing perceptions, thoughts, individual life challenges, personal testimonies and spiritual questions related to their day-to-day lives. An initial writing assignment was given in the form of an essay that addressed, "What attracts me to this group."

The researcher also began to provide teaching about leadership and biblical principles and introduced John Maxwell's leadership principles and Stephen Covey's *Seven Habits of Highly Effective Leaders.* One-on-one mentoring was also started through telephone prayer and consultation, and in-person meetings.

January 2013 – June 2013:

The researcher introduced prophetic demonstrations, and individual teaching assignments were started. Participants were introduced to opportunities to volunteer for service activities and to help with Sunday worship services (eight participants actually joined the church during this period).

Additional written assignments were given, which eventually developed into a booklet and study guide written to emerging adults with essays written by the participants. Participants were taught how to research and study scripture, and how to recognize the spiritual movement of God. Emphasis during this time was on prayer, but participants were choosing to engage in various church events such as Feed North County, Wellspring Foot Washing Service, Youth Shut-in, and the Youth Roundtable Spiritual Discussion service. They also chose to travel to a United Methodist-sponsored College Age Ministry Leadership Training seminar in Columbia, MO., (April 2013) and visited several churches where the pastor of the church was the speaker (May and June 2013).

July 2013 – October 2013:

The researcher administered a twelve-month survey in August 2013, continued teaching assignments, small group meetings and spiritual gift demonstrations, and written assignments such as, "How do I feel about church," or "What does this group ministry mean to me?" In October 2013, participants hosted "Healed to Serve," a healing service that provided a public forum to practice their gifts and talents, increase intimate relationships with the rest of the church members and build both leadership characteristics and loyalty to the overall church. Several participants were given speaking roles, while others recited prayers, prayed for people at the altar or exercised their prophetic gifts.

November – August 2014:

Small group discussion continued, but participants were asked to lead discussions by teaching about a biblical character assigned to them by the mentor, and they were asked to complete a lengthier spiritual gifts assessment form and another survey to highlight those things that they believed helped to increase their commitment to church and God.

Project Summary and Conclusions

The research group, affectionately called "Yes to God," was initiated because the researcher believed that allowing young adults to understand and discover their identities in God would help to create in them a new desire to commit to both church and God. Personal experiences as a young adult were buoyed by research before embarking on the project journey. The researcher believed that an experimental research project such as this, focused on young adults going through an open process of forming ideas and opinions, would reach the intended goals. This project, focused on Holy Spirit gift identification and activation, mentoring and leadership training, would help them embrace a connectedness to God and the church, and act on that acknowledgement in ways that indicated stronger commitment to both God and the church. Research results over the course of this study indicate that this project might well be an effective vehicle to increase interest in and commitment to the church and God, specifically in young adults. While the results may not yield to duplication in all contexts and within all age groups, they are encouraging as a means to maintain and grow church membership. Positive and traceable responses to gift identification and ignition elements, as well as mentoring and leadership teaching, delivered very positive outcomes that will hopefully inform and guide future efforts by church leaders to attract and retain young adults. There were many successful outcomes of the project.

While it was not a direct measurement within the project, it is worthy to note that an affinity was created and maintained among the study participants. Throughout the study and starting at month fourteen, the participants began to communicate outside of the group, planning activities together, praying and studying the Bible together, sharing job information, and in general being supportive of each other. Initially, this was done in segregated "clicks" of participants, but eventually by the project's end, all were included. This inclusive "group" capitalizes on this age group's focus on relating to individuals on a more personal level and exploring their relationships, as outlined by developmental psychologist Erik Erickson, whose work helped to inform the project.

The search for interpersonal competence, as outlined in Arthur Chickering's, *"Seven Vectors of Identity Development,"* also informed these outcomes. The participants were noted to be in a period of life within which their interpersonal competence involved listening, cooperating, and communicating effectively, but also they were developing the ability to tune in to another person and respond appropriately and to align their own agendas with group goals. At one time or another, each of the group members displayed this tendency to view themselves as part of a larger whole, as opposed to individually. This thought process helped to increase their later association as part of the church, or part of the workers for God. It no longer was simply about their wants and needs, but they learned to think and participate as part of a larger group, one necessary element in church membership and service to God.

One outcome that was measured within the survey data was church attendance and membership, and participation in church activities. Church attendance and participation was tracked by the number of those who regularly attended church, as well as those who ultimately became members. While attendance records for church service initially showed relatively low numbers, all participants attended an average of twice each month, with seven attending every Sunday morning. Of those who were attending twice each month, three expressed that they were concerned about their lack of attendance, and planned to improve. One actually did show improvement by the end of the study.

By the termination point of the study group, each participant also was consistently giving or tithing consistently to the church. Those that did not attend frequently brought tithes and offerings each time that they attended. That was a milestone among the group since at the beginning initial surveys suggested that most of them were unchurched, expressed a disdain for church people and church attendance, or chose not to even entertain the idea of attending church, and definitely not becoming members. By the end of the project, nine of the ten individuals had become members of the church. The remaining participant did not join the church, but still attended on occasion and currently continues to seek out the researcher/minister for prayer, ministry and opportunities for event participation. They also continue to express an interest in joining another church, and in continuing the research project as an ongoing ministry.(Which effectively has come to fruition with the creation of Rose of Sharon Ministries, Inc. in 2015) These results correspond directly to a final survey administered in month twenty-four that indicated a stronger understanding of theological principles, respect and appreciation of both God and the church, and a strong interest in continuing to learn about their gifts, God and the church overall.

Participation in church activities was strong among group members as well. A majority of them attended events to support the church youth groups, such as an evening of prayer, and a back to school lock-in. Additionally, several of the members helped to serve food on Thanksgiving, attended a church strategic planning meeting, and attended church anniversary, Thanksgiving service and other events. In fact, all of the members participated in two Healing Services, sponsored by the group in October of 2013 and October 2014, and four actually started and participate in a dance ministry for the church.

Participation and attendance at small group meetings where much of the leadership training and mentoring occurs, was consistent and regular for the most part. From the beginning, all of the participants committed to attending the meetings twice each month, even requesting that we meet three times during several of those months. Not only did they attend the meetings, they were active participants, taking on the roles of teacher when assigned, asking probing questions about God and theological principles and totally committing to the process of gift identification and activation.

Participants also demonstrated an increased commitment to the work of God in their lives by being actively engaged and engaging others during the small group meetings. Written essays and comments made during these meetings substantiate results that indicate an investment in these areas. Initial surveys indicated that while about 80% of the group members had been raised in church or at least by adults who taught them some biblical principles, almost none of them were interested in attending church at the initial start of the research group. Surveys, essays and participation numbers indicate that these attitudes have drastically changed, with many of the members confessing a desire to continue the group and attempting to recruit additional members to participate.

All ten participants still have full connectivity to the group, although two of them initially attended somewhat inconsistently. These individuals also, however, maintained contact with the researcher and other group members, seeking prayer and support and eventually returning to the group full-time. A third participant left the group after she became pregnant, but returned soon after, and fully participated through August 2014.

Based on attendance, essays, comments made during small group meetings, observation and overall participation, the researcher believes that this research project could indeed help address a decline in church attendance among those in this age group. Identifying Holy Spirit gifts in participants was introduced to them as the basis for the group, while mentoring consisting of prayer, emotional support and support with employment or school, coupled with the teaching of leadership principles and opportunities to teach themselves, helped to undergird the initial efforts dealing with spiritual gifts. Each of the participants, to some degree, were able to achieve many milestones related to Chickering's Seven Vectors, including a greater identity, a stronger sense of purpose, intellectual and interpersonal competence and even managing emotions in favor of training to becoming moved by the Spirit of God and not their own emotions.

If applied within the appropriate context, there is a great chance that this project would prove beneficial to churches that need to increase the number of young adults who join and commit to their church. Not only would it prove beneficial to churches, it would also allow young adults to take the journey of truly discovering their God-given purpose and fulfilling those things that they were created to accomplish. In addition, this project can serve to help these young adults matriculate to full adulthood in a responsible and productive manner, and allow them theological guidance in navigating life's challenges that is not based on social position or luck.

However, to reach these individuals the church must once again embrace the Holy Spirit and the principles surrounding those gifts given by the Holy Spirit as expressed in Pauline Theology, Corinthians and Ephesians. They must become central to theology in order to attract, retain and essentially feed those who have turned away from the church, and in some instances, God.

APPENDIX A

SURVEY TOOLS

Initial Survey – August 2012

First Name:
Best way to contact you:
Email Address:

1. Have you ever belonged to a church-based group or attended a particular church on a regular basis?
2. If you have belonged to a church, why did you join? Are you still attending and if not, why did you stop attending?
3. What do you think is the purpose of attending church?
4. Do you remember learning about God or Jesus as a child or teenager? What do you remember being taught?
5. What do you know about God? What do you know about Jesus? What do you know about the Holy Spirit?
6. Do you understand God's purpose in the life of someone who believes in God?
7. What do you think is the difference between having God in your life and not having God in your life?
8. Why did you agree to come here today?
9. Are there specific questions that you have, which we can discuss during these meetings?
10. What would you say is your biggest challenge in life right now?
11. Did you know that God places gifts, talents and special abilities in every believer? Would you like to learn about your own gifts, talents and special abilities?
12. Are there meeting dates and times that work best for you?

12-month Survey - August 2013

First Name:
Best way to contact you:
Email Address:

1. How long have you participated in this group?

2. What did you hope to gain/learn by participating in Yes to God?

3. What have you actually gained or learned by participating in Yes to God?

4. Have any of your beliefs or ideas changed related to God or church, since you began to participate in this group? If yes, what specific ideas or beliefs?

5. What do you feel is the best thing about the group?

6. What are some things that should be improved or added to make it more effective?

7. Have you ever invited a friend or someone that you were acquainted with to attend church since participating in the group?

8. What type of activity or event do you think would help encourage others to join a group like this?

9. Have your feelings about God or church attendance and participation changed since being in the group? At what point did you notice this change, and what are the specific changes you noticed?

10. What was done in the group, if anything, that helped change your attitudes or ideas about God or church?

24-month – August 2014

First Name:
Best way to contact you:
Email Address:

1. Why did you initially come to Yes to God? Number 1st, 2nd, 3rd
    A. Get closer to God
    B. Looking for a church to attend
    C. Felt empty and thought this might help
    D. Attracted by the idea of understanding my relationship to God and my spiritual gifts
    E. Just came with a friend
    F. Looking for something and didn't know what, but YTG seems to have it
    G. Other comments - please write them down

2. Why do you keep attending Yes to God? Number 1st, 2nd and 3rd
    A. Boyfriend/Girlfriend won't let me quit
    B. Spiritual mentoring/Mentor
    C. I am learning my gifts and what makes me special
    D. Learning how to operate in my spiritual gifts
    E. I am excited about learning to hear God's voice
    F. I like Wellspring folks
    G. I like learning about God's Word and how it can help me through life
    H. Other reasons (Please list)

3. Do you belong to a church?
    A. Nope and don't want to. Why?
    B. Yes. Why?
    C. Thinking about it
    D. Yes, but don't attend much. Why?

4. How do you feel about belonging to a church? Is your attitude about church any different that it was a year ago?

5. Do you think Yes to God was worth your time?
6. What would stop you from attending Yes to God?

APPENDIX B

ESSAYS/WRITTEN TESTIMONIALS

Essay One

I didn't even think about going to church during this part of my life because I left for college. I know that every church can treat you differently, so I wasn't ready for what I might find.

Before I went off to college, I joined a nice, friendly church. Everyone embraced me and showed me unconditional love (so I thought). While I was there, I learned a lot about God and how to pray and enter into his presence. Then near graduation time, things started to get a little different, but they were still nice and giving me gifts. Finally, when it was time for me to leave they told me that we could have live chats during prayer services and they even prayed for me before I left.

The first time I went back home everyone embraced me and gave me words of encouragement before I left, but when I returned again after a few months at school, it was like I was the devil himself when I walked into the church. They made me feel like I was wrong for going away to college: I felt like as long as I was attending school "out there" I wasn't good enough to be a part of their church. I asked myself, "where are the hugs, the words of encouragement, the same people that just told me they loved me like a sister?

It may have been that I just didn't fit anymore.

I stopped attending church for a while after that because I didn't like that feeling. I felt like everybody was more advanced than me; that I wasn't holy enough to worship with them.

There was one lady that never treated me that way though. She was always there if I needed to talk. She even encouraged me to begin my own prayer group while I was away at school and I did it. The girls in my dorm loved it, because they wanted that same connection with God that I did.

One day while I was in town, she called me and said "You should come visit my church. " My sister talked about it all the time, so I said "let me go see."

It was great. I loved the preached word and the lady was very happy to see me and I was happy to see her.

After I returned home from school for good, I just kept visiting the church since I lived in the area. One day the lady came up to me and my sister and said you all should come to our "Yes to God" (YTG) meetings. I didn't know what that was, but I was willing to follow her "till the wheels fell off" because I knew she was a true woman of God.

I attended one class and I didn't know what to think. I walked into the class like a "miss know it all" with my bible like I was going to teach them something. Little did I know that they were teaching classes, giving prophetic words to each other and conducting a whole lot of other Holy-spirit led-activities.

I thought this was amazing because they were just like me. One girl even told me that at first she thought I was the "I sleep with my bible type of girl."

Meeting them and coming to YTG is what has really kept me running to God. Now I know when God is speaking to me and I can give prophetic words to people that God directs me to speak to. I thank God for that lady (If she reads this she will know she is the one). If it wasn't for her, I don't think I would have ever found a great new church home or discovered the gifts that God has placed within me.

Essay Two

I didn't ever feel like church was a safe zone for me; that's why I didn't want to join. I felt as if I would be judged, and I would not feel comfortable. I just felt like I would not fit in and it just was not the place for me.

Growing up I was taught that we had to go to church every Sunday, and I did not understand why I had to go to listen to people that I did not understand teach me about a Bible that I didn't understand, in order to be a child of God; in order to be saved?

I had a lot of questions, too. If this is the house of the Lord, then why can't I feel comfortable? Do I have to go to church to go to heaven? I had so many questions with no answers, so I stayed away.

I thought that I would rather go to the club, where I fit in, where I wasn't judged, and where there are other people just like me…lost.

Something in my heart always had a passion for God no matter where I was or what I was doing. He has always been on my mind, in my heart and in my spirit. So, eventually, I could not resist it anymore. I responded to a request from my friend to come to church, and then joined the YTG group, and I haven't looked back. I am working in my spiritual gifts and enjoying my journey with God. I also have brought a lot of others into the YTG group as well.

Essay Three

I did not like church and never thought that I would ever go back because as a child, my mother forced my sisters and I to go. We use to be there all day. I was a kid and I didn't even know what this man was talking about. I just knew he just wouldn't stop talking. I was happy when I found out that they were starting a children's church; I lit up like a Christmas tree when I was told.

As I got older I saw people start to leave the church and then new people came. Other people started talking about them. My mother eventually took us out of that church, but by this time I was a teenager and was trying to "kick it." I wasn't worried about that place called "church." I use to spend the night at my friend's house just so I wouldn't have to go. When my friends and I started to praise dance and we came up with a name for our dance team, we were then inspired to attend church again.

There were 6-8 girls in the group, but we all grew up. Some had kids. Others went to college, but, I fell madly in love with another female. I would do anything for her. I fought my family and didn't care what people thought or had to say. When we moved in together, all Hell broke loose. I was cheating on her, she was cheating on me. We started fighting a lot. She started lying about the smallest things. I knew that it was time for us to move on. I ended up moving away with a family member.

Though the girl and I were still talking, I started talking to this guy I worked with. He was very sweet to me and gave me everything I wanted. He felt so perfect and it felt so right to be with him until I found I was pregnant. He couldn't deal with it at all and wanted me to abort "it" as if we didn't make this baby together. Long story short, no baby and no him.

I had hit rock bottom and I was under the "rock," until I talked to my best friend and she took me to a church. It was very small but it was cool because everyone in there was my age or a little older. I thought that I had found a new home. People were so nice and everybody was friendly. I was even on the praise dance team.

One day, though, people started leaving the church again. They started asking us to do things that I had never heard of and people started acting differently. So, I slowly started pushing my way out of the church. I didn't show up for some of the meetings or classes and really wasn't there on Sundays. One day I really wanted to go to church because I had a very bad week, but I didn't have any gas in my car. I ended up going to a church right down the street from my house.

When I say "we had church that day," we had it. I walked out of that church and felt like a new person. I felt like I could smile again, I could be myself again, and not have to worry about anything.

Now I'm in a college-age ministry group called "Yes to God" and I love it. They made me feel important, taught me that there are other people going through rough times. They taught me to pray always. I learned that if you feel like you can't do anything else, you should just pray.

Essay Four

I didn't want to attend church at first because I didn't really see anybody at the church that was my age and people who had gone to church before made it seem like we had to do it; just because "it was the right thing to do." They never really cared if I believed in God or not; they just wanted to see people coming to church. Now, I can't say that this is true of all churches, but I think it is true of most of them.

Another reason why I didn't want to attend church was because I never had anyone to really explain to me what church really was and to really teach me about God. They never took time to help me understand who God was and why God put us on Earth, but I always believed in God.

Finally, I thought that if I didn't give money, I wasn't doing the right thing, but most of that has changed now. I joined YTG and then I joined Wellspring Church this year on my own. No one forced me to walk to the altar. No one threatened me with going to Hell. I made a choice and I don't regret it.

Essay Five

I was confused about God during the majority of my childhood. I grew up a Christian, going to church with my mom, and hating getting up early to go. I listened though and I tried my best to understand, but I didn't understand.

The confusion really came when my dad tried to teach me about the Muslim religion. I am not one of those Christians who will "put down" other religions, but I choose to be a Christian and my beliefs do not align with the Muslim religion. My dad totally confused me, not saying he was teaching me bad things, but he made me confused about what beliefs went with what religion. I was very young and curious about a ton of things. I had gotten so confused and curious; I even went as far as studying all religions, even Satanism.

I shortly became extremely depressed and even tried to commit suicide at 17. That is also when I renewed my faith in Jesus Christ.

Everyone was stunned by my new behaviors and beliefs! I was a new person! I was confident and I loved myself! This was my start of speaking into people's lives as a prophetess, and it was life changing. God started to use me in so many ways!

I have a gift of dreaming and God is able to speak to me in dreams. I am able to warn other people of what's to come, however, some people's reactions are not so welcoming sometimes. Some claimed I was a physic or did the devil's work, but they're wrong!

A lot of people don't understand that God puts gifts in all of us! Not everyone is capable of doing the same thing or even at the same level, but God put something special in all of us! The question is, how do you tap into that gift? "Yes to God" has helped me tap into my gift in levels I'd never imagined! I am only 20 now so just imagine if I keep myself aligned with God's will where will I be? Only God knows, and I cannot wait for God to move me and use me. So what are you waiting for? God has gifts just for you with your name on it! Now own them!

Essay Six

The first time that I felt that God actually could have called me to be both a prophet and a preacher, I was shocked. I kept thinking to myself, "God has given me these gifts that allow me to tell people what God tells me to share with them, words that lift them up, and to spread the Word of God." I thought of what a blessing that was.

Sometimes I just can't believe it and then I start to question it. What if I'm not really hearing from God? What if I am only saying just what's on my own mind and not the right things? What if people don't "feel" what I am saying? This is what I said before.

Now, I truly believe that God has given me this gift and I am going to use it and spread it as far and wide as God dictates. It is a lot or work, but I am ready.

Essay Seven

To describe what it feels like to finally say "yes," to connecting with God is easy for me. It is especially easy when I am in church.

Has there ever been a time when you were sitting in church listening to the preacher, and everything that he or she was saying seemingly was directed toward you?

There were times at Wellspring when I have been listening to the preacher, and it seemed like he was talking directly to me. It is especially true of our preacher because he is so transparent. He says what he means and shares a lot.

That makes me feel good because I know that I am not the only one who has problems or the only one who is going through some challenges. I think that is a blessing.

It is also a gift from God. How can someone that you have never talked to about your problems, pretty much say what's on your mind and how you feel?

That's what saying "Yes," feels like to me; like God is giving me personal attention to help me get through this life.

Essay Eight

Control has always been a big issue for me. I am a "take charge" person, and some say I can be like a steam roller. When I see something that I want or think that I need, I simply make it happen.

Working hard comes naturally to me, but I am learning that if your hard work is not aligned with God's purposes it can be in vain. We can sometimes work much harder because we do not trust God and have not allowed him to guide us. I struggle with letting God control situations because I don't feel completely comfortable giving up control. Allowing God to control situations sometimes can make me nervous, impatient, and frustrated.

Recently though, I truly accepted God into my life and although I still struggle with control sometimes, I get through it. I've seen the outcome of both ways of acting and accepting God instead of fighting God is the path that I want to travel.

By letting God take the reins, things come easier at times, my stress level has gone down and I enjoy my life more than I have before. God has given me the ability to truly see the good in life again.

Essay Nine

I was once told by a pastor that I am a child of God and that God is working on me. I was always taught that in order to be saved, you had to get the Holy Ghost or speak in tongues and I was never that person.

Joining "Yes to God" has taught me that those things are not necessarily true. I do not have to go to church every Sunday, I can still listen to Rap and Rhythm and Blues music. I can still have a drink of wine sometimes and I can wear what I want.

Being saved has nothing to do with those things. God doesn't care about that. He cares about your relationship with him and the work He put you on this earth to do. All of the rest eventually takes care of itself if you follow Him. That freed me from trying to be a person that I never thought I could be for God.

I know what God needs me to do for Him. I am a leader and I lead by example. I know now that all things can be done by and through Christ. I have no more shame in who I am. I am not scared of going to church, and I'm not scared to fall on the floor and praise and worship God.

Yes to God has taught me who God is. It has taught me how to hear from God and communicate with God. It has taught me how to walk by the Word of God, and to stick by God's side.

Essay Ten

Absolutely everything has changed about me since I started attending church, starting with my personality to the choices I make on a day-to-day basis.

Ever since I began giving time to Wellspring and to the "Yes to God" group, I have evolved into the deeper side of myself and discovered who I really am inside of the shell I normally put myself in. I have found it easier to open up to others that I don't know, but before I would find it difficult and sometimes I would be very rigid when even just saying "hello" to people I didn't know.

Members of Wellspring as well as YTG have given me the love, loyalty and liability needed to freely express myself in order to grow a stronger relationship with God; especially through dancing and socializing with others my age, to gain relationships and understanding of common situations.

Being able to witness my own growth as a result of my involvement with the church and the group delights me, but hearing others tell me that they see me blossoming, tops it all off.

Personally, I have prayed more than I ever did, and I now realize that as long as I pray and keep faith in God, everything that's meant to be will be in line with God's will. In addition, I also find myself not giving up as easily in my relationships, especially the one with my long-time boyfriend. Our relationship has been put to the test multiple times, but when I find myself praying about it, things get better and I don't feel like giving up.

I am very pleased with the young woman that I am beginning to become and I feel so blessed to have such wonderful and beautiful people in my life to help me make and notice the transition in my life. I know I am not perfect and never will be and I have so much more spiritual growing to do, but I don't mind because I adore the journey. I look forward to many more experiences over the years to come.

Just as I had expressed to Ms. Nina before, I wouldn't ask to be a member of any other church or college-age group, because Wellspring and the "Yes to God" group have set a bar that none can reach.

Essay Eleven

"Yes to God" has changed me a lot and in many ways. I attend church more often, I am learning more about God and I now understand that God is the biggest thing in my life.

I also have grown as a young man and a son of God. With the help that I am getting these days, there is no telling what great plans God has for me.

"Yes to God" is one of the biggest challenges I have had in my life, but I can honestly say that the group has supported me and is a gift from God.

If I wasn't involved with the "Yes to God" group, there is no telling what I would be doing, so I thank God for it. I appreciate the group and I am just thankful that it is there, and that it is making me a better person than I ever was.

APPENDIX C

WAGNER-MODIFIED HOUTS QUESTIONNAIRE

STEP I: WAGNER-MODIFIED HOUTS QUESTIONNAIRE

For each statement, mark to what extent it is true of your life: MUCH, SOME, LITTLE, or NOT AT ALL.

	(3)	(2)	(1)	(0)
	Much	Some	Little	Not At All

1. I have a desire to speak direct messages from God that edify or exhort or comfort others.

2. I have enjoyed relating to a certain group of people over a long period of time, sharing personally in their successes and failures.

3. People have told me that I have helped them learn some biblical truth in a meaningful way.

4. I have applied spiritual truth effectively to situations in my own life.

5. Others have told me that I have helped them distinguish key and important facts of scripture.

6. I have verbally encouraged the wavering, the troubles or discouraged.

7. Others in the church have noted that I was able to see through phoniness before it was evident to other people.

8. I find I manage money well in order to give liberally to the Lord's work.

9. I have assisted Christian leaders to relieve them for their essential job.

10. I have a desire to work with those who have physical or mental problems, to alleviate their suffering.

11. I feel comfortable relating to ethnics and minorities, and they seem to accept me.

12. I have led others to a decision for salvation through faith in Christ.

13. My home is always open to people passing through who need a place to stay.

14. When in a group, I am often the one others often look to for vision and direction.

15. When I speak people seem to listen and agree.

16. In the name of the Lord, I have been used in curing diseases instantaneously.

17. I have spoken in tongues.

18. Sometimes when a person speaks in tongues, I get an idea about what God is saying.

19. I could live more comfortably, but I choose not to in order to live with the poor.

20. I am single and I enjoy it.

21. I spend at least an hour a day in prayer.

22. I have spoken to evil spirits and they have obeyed me.

23. I enjoy being called upon to do special jobs around the church.

24. Through God I have revealed specific things, which will happen in the future.

25. I have enjoyed assuming the responsibility for the spiritual well being of a particular group of Christians.

26. I feel I can explain the New Testament teaching about the health and ministry of the body of Christ in a relevant way.

27. I can intuitively arrive at solutions to fairly complicated problems.

28. I have had insights of spiritual truth which others have said helped bring them closer to God.

29. I can effectively motivate people to get involved in ministry when it's needed.

30. I can "see" the Spirit of God resting on certain people from time to time.

31. My giving records show that I give considerably more than 10 percent of my income to the Lord's work.

32. Other people have told me that I helped them become more effective in their ministries.

33. I have cared for others when they have had material or physical needs.

34. I feel I could learn another language well in order to minister to those in a different culture.

35. I have shared joyfully how Christ has brought me to Himself in a way that is meaningful to non-believers.

36. I enjoy taking charge of church suppers or social gatherings.

37. I have believed God for the impossible and have seen it happen in a tangible way.

38. Other Christians have followed my leadership because they believed in me.

39. I enjoy the details of organizing ideas, people, resources and time for more effective ministry.

40. God has used me personally to perform supernatural signs and wonders.

41. I enjoy praying for sick people because I know that many of them will be healed as a result.

42. I have spoken an immediate message of God to His people in a language that I have never learned.

43. I have interpreted tongues with the result that the body of Christ was edified, exhorted, or comforted.

44. Living a simple lifestyle is an exciting challenge for me.

45. Other people have noted that I feel more indifferent about not being married than most.

46. When I hear a prayer request, I pray for that need for several days at least.

47. I have actually heard a demon speak in a loud voice.

48. I don't have many special skills, but I do what needs to be done around the church.

49. People have told me that I have communicated timely and urgent messages, which have come directly from the Lord.

50. I feel unafraid of giving spiritual guidance and direction in a group of Christians.

51. I can devote considerable time to learning new biblical truths in order to communicate them to others.

52. When a person has a problem I can frequently guide them to the best Biblical solution.

53. Through study or experience I have discerned major strategies or techniques God seems to use in furthering His kingdom.

54. People come to me in their afflictions or suffering, and have told me that they have been helped, relieved and healed.

55. I can tell with a fairly high degree of assurance when a person is afflicted by an evil spirit.

56. When I am moved by an appeal to give to God's work, I usually find the money that I need to do it.

57. I have enjoyed doing routine tasks that led to more effective ministry by others.

58. I enjoy visiting in hospitals and/or retirement homes, and feel I do well in such a ministry.

59. People in a different race or culture have been attracted to me, and we have related well.

60. Non-Christians have noted that they feel comfortable when they are around me, and that I have a positive effect on them toward developing a faith in Christ.

61. When people come to our home, they indicate that they "feel at home" with us.

62. Other people have told me that I had faith to accomplish what seemed impossible to them.

63. When I set goals, others seem to accept them readily.

64. I have been able to make effective and efficient plans for accomplishing the goals of a group.

65. God regularly seems to do impossible things through my life.

66. Others have told me that God healed them of an emotional problem when I ministered to them.

67. I can speak to God in a language I have never learned.

68. I have prayed that I may interpret if someone begins speaking in tongues.

69. I am not poor but I can identify with poor people.

70. I am glad I have more time to serve the Lord because I am single.

71. Intercessory prayer is one of my favorite ways of spending time.

72. Others call on me when they suspect that someone is demonized.

73. Others have mentioned that I seem to enjoy routine tasks and do well at them.

74. I sometimes have a strong sense of what God wants to say to people in response to a particular situation.

75. I have helped fellow believers by guiding them to relevant portions of the Bible and praying with them.

76. I feel I can communicate Biblical truths to others and see resulting changes in knowledge, attitudes, values, or conduct.

77. Some people indicate that I have perceived and applied Biblical truth to the specified needs of fellow believers.

78. I study and read quite a bit in order to learn new Biblical truths.

79. I have a desire to effectively counsel the perplexed, the guilty or the addicted.

80. I can recognize whether a person's teaching is from God, from Satan, or of human origin.

81. I am so confident that God will meet my needs that I give to Him sacrificially and consistently.

82. When I do things behind the scenes and others are helped, I am joyful.

83. People call on me to help those who are less fortunate.

84. I would be willing to leave comfortable surroundings if it would enable me to share Christ with more people.

85. I get frustrated when others don't seem to share their faith with unbelievers as much as I do.

86. Others have mentioned to me that I am a very hospitable person.

87. There have been times when I have felt sure I knew God's specific will for the future growth of His work, even when others did not seem so sure.

88. When I join a group, others seem to back off and expect me to take the leadership.

89. I am able to give directions to others without using persuasion to get them to accomplish a task.

90. People have told me that I was God's instrument which brought supernatural changes in lives or circumstances.

91. I have prayed for others and physical healing has actually occurred.

92. When I give a public message in tongues, I expect it to be interpreted.

93. I have interpreted tongues in a way that seemed to bless others.

94. Others tell me I sacrifice much materially in order to minister.

95. I am single and I have little difficulty controlling my sexual desires.

96. Others have told me that my prayers for them have been answered in tangible ways.

97. Other people have been instantly delivered from demonic oppression when I have prayed.

98. I prefer being active and doing something rather than just sitting around talking or reading or listening to a speaker.

99. I sometimes feel that I know exactly what God wants me to do in ministry at a specific point in time.

100. People have told me that I have helped them to be restored to the Christian community.

101. Studying the Bible and sharing my insights with others is very satisfying for me.

102. I have felt an unusual presence of God and personal confidence when important

decisions needed to be made.

103. I have the ability to discover new truths for myself through reading or observing situations firsthand.

104. I have urged others to seek a Biblical solution to their affliction or suffering.

105. I can tell whether a person speaking in tongues is genuine.

106. I have been willing to maintain a lower standard of living in order to benefit God's work.

107. When I serve the Lord, I really don't care who gets the credit.

108. I would enjoy spending time with a lonely, shut-in person or someone in prison.

109. More than most, I have had a strong desire to see people of other countries won to the Lord.

110. I am attracted to non-believers because of my desire to win them to Christ.

111. I have desired to make my home available to those in the Lord's service whenever needed.

112. Others have told me that I am a person of unusual vision and I agree.

113. When I am in charge, things seem to run smoothly.

114. I have enjoyed bearing the responsibility for the success of a particular task within my church.

115. In the name of the Lord, I have been able to recover sight to the blind.

116. When I pray for the sick, either I or they feel sensations of tingling or warmth.

117. When I speak in tongues, I believe it is edifying to the Lord's body.

118. I have interpreted tongues in such a way that the message appeared to be directly from God.

119. Poor people accept me because I choose to live on their level.

120. I readily identify with Paul's desire for others to be single as he was.

121. When I pray, God frequently speaks to me, and I recognize His voice.

122. I cast out demons in Jesus' name.

123. I respond cheerfully when asked to do a job, even if it seems menial.

Appendix D

The following benchmarks provide guidance concerning establishment and maintenance of a college-aged ministry to each church and ministerial group, and establish a protocol for ensuring that each ministry group receives proper leadership and directions. Several of the benchmarks, such as the admonition not to use a ministry template and its emphasis on relationships indicate the United Methodist model for ministry is an open one, allowing room for each church to design its ministry based on the characteristics and demographics of its college-age participants.[156] Both the current members and future members of Wellsprings college-age ministry group are African American, this strategy will effectively allow for a model to be established that takes into consideration the concerns, needs, characteristics and cultural demographics concerning young African Americans.

Benchmarks for Missouri College-age Ministries[157]

1. **Know your campus/mission field.**
   Don't just use a template for ministry.

2. **Daily presence in the mission field.**
   This can be led by campus pastor or other leadership (student leaders, professors, other church members, etc.)

3. **Ministry is about people** not programs.

4. **Sustainability**
   Organic (connectional and continual) relationship with the church and college-age ministries

---

[156] Ibid.

[157] Ibid.

5. **Leadership development**
   College-age persons in college-age ministry
   College-age persons in over-all ministry of the church
   Lay College-age Ministry Team

6. **Finances**
   Fiscal accountability
   Develop financial support

7. **Relationships**
   Utilize an ongoing effective recruitment plan.
   In mission field
   Identify feeder systems (with high schools, youth groups, camps, etc.)

8. **Worship service**
   Engage college-age persons

9. **Intentional discipleship**
   Small groups, Bible study, mentoring, etc.

10. **Missional involvement**
    Within the community, outside of the community

11. **Lay College-Age Ministry Team**
    Hospitality in the church and in college-aged ministries

12. **Mentoring and connecting**
    Foster multigenerational involvement with congregation

13. **Coaching**

14. **College-age minister self-care**
    Take time for renewal. Spend time with God, family, friends, and other life-giving opportunities. Make continuing education a priority.

BIBLIOGRAPHY

Andrew, Richard. *Research Questions*. New York, NY: Bloomsbury Publishing, 2003.

Ammerman, Nancy T., and J.W. Carroll, C.S. Dudley, and W. McKinney. *Studying Congregations: A New Handbook*. Nashville, TN: Abingdon Press, 1998.

Arnett, Jenson, J. *Adolescence and Emerging Adulthood: A Cultural Approach 4th ed*. Upper Saddle River, NJ: Prentice Hall, 2010.

Barna, George. "Major Faith Shifts Evident Among Whites, Blacks, and Hispanics Since 1991." *State of the Church August 2011 Report.* (August 2, 2011). Accessed November 24, 2013. http://www.barna.org/faith-spirituality/510-major-faith-shifts-evident-among-whites-blacks-and-hispanics-since-1991#.U9Bx4hDRYSo.

_____. *Grow Your Church from the Outside: Understanding the Unchurched and How to Reach Them*. Ventura, CA: Regal 2002.

Barrick, Audrey, "Reasons Why Young Adults Quit Church." *The Christian Post,* August 8, 2007. Accessed November 23, 2012. http://www.christianpost.com/news/survey-reasons-why-young-adults-quit-church-28813/.

Barth, Karl. "The Doctrine of God." *Church Dogmatics*, vol. II, Part I, eds. G.W. Bromiley and T. F. Torrance. London: T and T Clark, 1957.

_____. *The Epistle of the Romans,* Translated by Edwyn C. Hoskins. London, England: Oxford University Press, 1933.

Beck, Laura E. *Development Through the Lifespan*. Normal, IL: Illinois State University, 2009.

Bellini, Peter J. *Truth Therapy: Renewing Your Mind with the Word of God*. Maitland, FL: Xulon Press, 1996.

Bettenson, Henry and Chris Maunder. *Documents of the Christian Church*. 4th ed. New York, NY: Oxford University Press, 2011.

Bevere, John. *The Bait of Satan: Living Free from the Deadly Trap of Offense*. Lake Mary, FL: Charisma House, 2004.

Bomar, Chuck. *College Ministry from Scratch*. Grand Rapids, MI: Zondervan, 2010.

Bonhoeffer, Dietrich. *The Cost of Discipleship*. New York, NY: The Macmillan Company, 1949.

Bowman, R. M. *Why Should You Believe in the Trinity?* Grand Rapids, MI: Baker Book House, 1989.

Brueggemann, Walter. "The Book of Jeremiah: Portrait of the Prophet." *Interpretation* 37, no. 2, (April 1983):130-145 *ATLASerials, Religion Collection*, EBSCO*host.* Accessed March 19, 2013. http://search.ebscohost.com/login.aspx?direct=true&db=a6h&AN=ATLA0000929117&site=ehost-live

Buttrick, George A. ed. "1 Timothy: The Divine Commission." Vol. 11. *The Interpreter's Bible Library in Twelve Volumes,* Nashville, TN: Abingdon Press, 1955.

Buckingham, Marcus and Donald O. Clifton. *Now, Discover Your Strengths*. New York, NY: The Free Press, 2001.

Chessire, Barbara. *The Best Dissertation…A Finished Dissertation*. Portland, OR: National Book Co., 1993.

CityTown.info.com. Accessed September 15, 2012. http://www.citytowninfo.com/places/missouri/ferguson.

Clapp, Rodney. *A Peculiar People: The Church as Culture in Post Christian Society*. Downers Grove, IL: IVP, 1996.

Clark, David, K. and Robert Rakestraw, V. *Readings in Christian Ethics.* Vol. 2: *Issues and Applications.* Grand Rapids, MI: Baker Academic, 1996.

Cobb, John. *Christ in a Pluralist Age*. Philadelphia, PA: Westminster Press, 1975.

Conger, Jay Alden. *Spirit at Work: Discovering the Spirituality in Leadership*. San Francisco, CA: Jossey-Bass, 1994.

Crabtree, T.T. "Prophet's call (Jeremiah)-a dialogue with God." *Southwestern Journal of Theology* 4, no. 1 (1961): 33-56 ATLA Serials, Religion Collection, EBSCOhost Accessed March 19, 2013. http://search.ebscohost./com/login.aspx?direct=true&db=a6h&AN=ATLA0000684746&site=host-live.

Craigie, Peter C., Kelley Page H. and Drinkard, Joel F. Jr. *Jeremiah*. Vol. 26, *World Bible Commentary*. Dallas, TX: Word Books, 1991.

Cranton, Patricia. *Professional Developmental as Transformative Learning: New Perspectives for Teachers of Adults.* San Francisco, CA: Jossey-Bass, A Wiley Company, 1996.

Creswell, John W. *Research Design: Qualitative, Quantitative, and Mixed Methods Approaches*. Thousand Oaks, CA: Sage Publishing, 2009.

Daloz, Laurent A. *Effective Teaching and Mentoring: Realizing the Transformational Power of Adult Learning Experiences*. San Francisco, CA: Jossey-Bass, 1986.

Denio, Francis B. "The scriptural teaching respecting the Holy Spirit." *Journal of BiblicalLiterature* vol. 15, no.1-2 (January 1,1896):135-150. Accessed March 7, 2013. *ATLASerials, Religion Collection*, EBSCO*host* http://search.ebscohost.com/login.aspx?direct=true&db=a6h&AN=ATLA0001282349&site=ehost-live.

DeYoung, Kevin. *Just Do Something: A Liberating Approach to Finding God's Will.* Chicago, IL: Moody Publishers, 2009.

Dillon, Pamela K. *Encounters with Leadership-Producing and Promoting Healthy Leaders: Handbook and Manual of Mentorship and Fellowship*. Bloomington, IL: Westbow Press, 2013.

_____. *The Greater Yes: Answering the Call of God*. Indianapolis, IN: Wordclay Publishing, 2009.

Dominy, Bert. "Paul and spiritual gifts: reflections on 1 Corinthians 12-14." *Southwestern Journal of Theology* 26, no. 1(1983):49-68. Accessed 7, 2013. *ATLASerials, Religion Collection*, EBSCO*host*

> http://search.ebscohost.com/login.aspx?direct=true&db=a6h&AN=ATLA0001282349&site=ehost-live.

Douglas, Julie M. "Reflections on divine revelation and personal encounter with the Lord." *AFER: African Ecclesial Review* 42, no. 3-4: (1982):151-155. accessed April 7, 2013. *ATLA Religion Database and ATLASerials,* EBSCO*host* http://search.ebscohost.com/login.aspx?direct=true&db=rfh&AN=ATLA0001281173&site=ehost-live.

Fowler, James. *The Psychology of Human Development and the Quest for Meaning.* New York, NY: Harper One, 1995.

_____. *Becoming Adult: Becoming Christian.* San Francisco, CA: Jossey-Boss, 1999.

Garcia, Alberto L. "Spiritual Gifts and the work of the Kingdom." *Concordia Theological Quarterly* 49, no. 2-3 (1985):149-160. Accessed April 28, 2013. *ATLASerials, Religion Collection*, EBSCO*host* http://search.ebscohost.com/login.aspx?direct=true&db=a6h&AN=ATLA0000959480&site=ehost-live.

Gonzalez, Justo L. *Essential Theological Terms.* Louisville, KY: John Knox Press, 2005.

_____. *The Story of Christianity: The Reformation to the Present Day.* New York, NY: Harper One, 2010.

_____. *The Story of Christianity: The Early Church to the Dawn of the Reformation.* New York, NY: Harper One, 2010.

Gorman, Michael J. *Elements of Biblical Exegesis: A Basic Guide for Students and Ministers.* Peabody, IL: Hendrickson Publishers, 2001.

Greenwood, Davyd J. and Morten Levin. *Introduction to Action Research: Social Research for Social Change.* Thousand Oaks, CA: SAGE Publications Inc., 1998.

Guzik, David. "1 Timothy." *David Guzik's Commentaries on the Bible.* Accessed March 25, 2012. http://www.studylight.org/com/guz/print.cgi?bk=53&ch=6&vs=1.

Haight, Roger. "Spirituality and Social Justice Making: A Christological Perspective." *Spirituality Today* 34, no. 4 (Winter 1982): 312-325. Accessed March 12, 2013. http://www.spiritualitytoday.org/spir2day/823443haight.html.

Harper, Nile. "Charitable Choice: A Theological Perspective." Winter 2001. *ATLASerials, Religion Collection*, EBSCO*host* Accessed March 1, 2013. http://www.ebscohost.com/ehost/detail?sid=3ba15c53-acbb-4b6d-96ff-f676c360d5f9%40sessionmgr15&vid=1&hid=8&bdata=JnNpdGU9ZWhvc3QtbG12ZQ%3d%3d#db=f5h&AN=4238444.

Hayford, W. Jack. *The Hayford Study Bible Handbook: The Complete Companion for Spirit-Filled Bible Study*. Nashville, TN: Thomas Nelson, Inc. 1995.

Heath, Gordon, L. *Doing Church History: A User Friendly Introduction to Researching the History of Christianity.* Toronto, Canada: Clements Publishing, 2008.

Hendrix, John and Lloyd Householder, eds. *The Equipping of Disciples.* Nashville, TN: Broadman Press, 1977.

Henry, Matthew. "Matthew Henry Commentary on the Whole Bible." *BibleStudyTools.* Accessed March 13, 2013. http://www.biblestudytools.com/commentaries/matthew-henry-complete/1-timothy/.

Hilber, John W. "Diversity of OT Prophetic Phenomena and NT Prophecy." *Westminster Theological Journal* 56, no. 2 (Fall 1994): 243-258. *ATLASerials, Religion Collection*, EBSCO*host.* Accessed April 28, 2013. http://search.ebscohost.com/login.aspx?direct=true&db=a6h&AN=ATLA0000885966&site=ehost-live.

Hocken, Peter. "Jesus Christ and the Gifts of the Spirit." *Pneuma* 5, no. 1 (Spring 1983):1-16. *ATLASerials, Religion Collection*, EBSCO*host*. Accessed March 7, 2013. http://search.ebscohost.com/login.aspx?direct=true&db=a6h&AN=ATLA0000930639&site=ehost-live.

Howard, Shannon. "After 124 years, Ferguson United Methodist Closes Its Doors." *NOCO The Online Magazine of North St. Louis County,* 2012. October 27, 2010. Accessed December 9, 2012. http://nocostl.com/?s=Ferguson+United+Methodist+Church&x=0&y=).

Huizenga, Leroy. "How Do Churches Grow." *First Things First Magazine*. Institute on Religion and Public Life. (July 12, 2012). Accessed on March 2012.
http://www.firstthings.com/onthesquare/2012/07/how-do-churches-grow.

Humphreys, Fisher. "The Revelation of the Trinity." *Perspectives in Religious Studies* 33, no. 3 (Fall 2006):285-303. *ATLASerials, Religion Collection*, EBSCO*host.* Accessed March 7, 2012. http://search.ebscohost.com/login.aspx?direct=true&db=a6h&AN=ATLA0001557908&site=ehost-live.

Jamieson, Robert A. R. Fausset and David Brown. "1 Timothy 3" in *Commentary: Critical and Explanatory of the Whole Bible.* Graceworks Multimedia. September 17, 2008. Kindle version.

Johnson, Benton, Dean R. Hoge and Donald A. Luidens, "Mainline Churches: The Real Reason for Decline," *First Things First Magazine*, 31 (March, 1993):13-18. Accessed November 24, 2013. http://www.leaderu.com/ftissues/ft9303/articles/johnson.html.

Kellar, Marcel. *Timothy, Stir Up Your Gift*. Nashville, TN: MegaCorporation, 2001.

MacMullen, Ramsay. *Christianizing the Roman Empire*. New Haven, CT: Yale University Press, 1984.

Mann, Thomas. *The Oxford Guide to Library Research*, 3rd ed., New York, NY: Oxford University Press, 2004.

Maxwell, John. C. *The 21 Irrefutable Laws of Leadership*. Nashville, TN: Thomas Nelson, 2007.

McCallum, Dennis. *Members of One Another: How to Build a Biblical Ethos into your Church.* Houston, TX: New Paradigm Publishing, 2010.

McCann, Vincent. *What is the Significance of the Doctrine of the Trinity for Living the Christian Life,* Spotlight Ministries, 2000. Accessed November 23, 2013. www.spotlightministries.org.uk.

McCorn, Lester Agyei. *Standing on Holy Common Ground: An Africentric Ministry Approach to Prophetic Community Engagement.* Chicago, IL: MMGI Books, 2013.

McGrath, Alister E. *Christian Theology: An Introduction.* Kings College, NJ: John Wiley & Sons, 2011.

McNiff, Jean, Pamela Lomax and Jack Whitehead. *You and Your Action Research Project.* New York, NY: Routledge-Farmer, 2003.

Menzies, Alan D., ed. *Latin Christianity: Its Founder, Tertullian.* Vol. 3 of *The Anti-Nicene Fathers: Translations of the Writings of the Fathers Down to AD 325.*Christian Classical Ethereal Library. Accessed November 10, 2013. http://www.ccel.org/ccel/schaff/anf03.toc.html#P334_131093.

Miller, Patrick D., ed. *Jeremiah.* Vol. VI. *The New Interpreter's Bible A Commentary in Twelve Volumes.* Nashville, TN: Abingdon Press, 1994.

Moore, Carey A. *Daniel, Esther and Jeremiah; The Additions.* Garden City, NJ: Doubleday and Company, Inc. 1977.

Mous, Bill. *"Prophetic Social Justice Making,"* Ontario, Canada: Anglican Diocese of Niagara, 2009. Accessed November 24, 2012. http://www.niagara.anglican.ca/vision/socialjustice.cfm.

Mouw Richard J. "Carl Henry Was Right," *Christianity Today Magazine,* (27 January, 2010). Accessed November 2, 2012. http://www.christianitytoday.com/ct/2010/january/25.30.html?paging=off.

MOVOTO LLC. "Neighborhood Information for Ferguson, MO 63135." Accessed December 1, 2012. http://www.movoto.com/neighborhood/mo/ferguson/63135.htm#rentalInformationSection.

Myer, Ron. *Five Fold Ministry Made Practical.* Lititz, PA: House to House Publications, 2006.

Myers, A.C., *The Eerdmans Bible Dictionary*. Grand Rapids, MI:Eerdmans, 1987.

Myers, Joyce. *How to Hear from God: Learn to Know His Voice and Make Right Decisions*. Nashville, TN: Faithworks, 2008.

Myers, William R. *Research in Ministry: Primer for the Doctor of Ministry Program*. Chicago, IL: Exploration Press, 2001.

Nees, Thomas. *Compassion Evangelism: Meeting Human Needs*. Kansas City, MO: Beacon Hill Press, 1996.

O'Connor, Kathleen M. "The Prophet Jeremiah and Exclusive Loyalty to God." *Interpretation* 59, no. 2 (April 2005):130-140. *ATLA Religion Database with ATLASeries*, EBSCO*host*. Accessed March 19, 2013. http://search.ebscohost.com/login.aspx?direct=true&db=rfh&AN=ATLA0001455228&site=ehost-live.

Overholt, Thomas W. "Jeremiah." *Harper Collins Bible Commentary*. New York, NY, Harper Collins, 1988.

Painter, John. "The Charismatic Movement and the New Testament." *Journal of Theology for Southern Africa*. No. 7 (1974):50-60. ATLASerials, Religion Collection, EBSCOhost 9. Accessed March 7, 2013. http://searach.ebscphost.com/login.aspx?direct=true&db=a6h&AN=ATLA0000724301&site=ehost-live.

Parks, Sharon D. *Big Questions, Worthy Dreams: Mentoring Emerging Adults in their Search for Meaning, Purpose and Faith*. San Francisco, CA: Jossey-Bass, Inc. 2011.

Perman, Matt. "What is the Doctrine of the Trinity." DesiringGod. Last modified January 23, 2006. Accessed November 26, 2012. http://www.desiringgod.org/resource-library/articles/what-is-the-doctrine-of-the-trinity.

_____. "Why Sound Doctrine Leads to Effective Action for Good." Desiring God. Last modified November 12, 2010. Accessed November 22, 2012. http://www.churchleaders.com/pastors/pastor-articles/146212-why-sound-doctrine-leads-to-action.html.

Pew Research Center, 2009, Religious Landscape Study, November 9, 2009, http://www.pewresearch.org/2009/11/09/religious-landscape-survey-data-release/

Pew Research Center, 2014 Religious Landscape Study, June 4 – September 30, 2015 http://www.pewforum.org/2015/11/03/chapter-1-importance-of-religion-and-religious-beliefs/

Pohly, Kenneth. *Transforming the Rough Places: The Ministry of Supervision.* Franklin, TN: Providence House Publishers, 2001.

Proctor, Samuel DeWitt. *The Substance of Things Hoped For: A Memoir of African-American Faith.* Valley Forge, PA: Judson Press, 1999.

Purkey, Edward, ed. "The Sermons of John Wesley-Sermon 89: The More Excellent Way" *Wesley Center Online from Wesley Center for Applied Theology at Northwest Nazarene University* (1999). Accessed March 24, 2013. http://wesley.nnu.edu/john-wesley/the-sermons-of-john-wesley-1872-edition/sermon-89-the-more-excellent-way/.

Rainer, Thomas S. III and Sam S. Rainer. *Essentail Church: Reclaiming a Generation of Dropouts.* Nashville, TN: B & H Publishing Group, 2008.

Rev. Alexander Roberts and James Donaldson, ed. *Latin Christianity, Its Founder, Tertullain, The Writings of the Fathers Down to AD 325.* Vol. 10. Buffalo, NY: The Christian Literature Publishing Company, 1885-96.

Ruffing, Janet K. *Mysticism and Social Transformation.* Syracuse, NY: Syracuse University Press, 2001.

Setran, David P. and Chris A. Kielsing. "*Spiritual Formation in Emerging Adults: A Practical Theology for College and Young Adult Ministry.* Grand Rapids, MI: Baker Academic, 2013.

Smith, Barry D. "The Holy Spirit in Pauline Theology: The New Testament and its Context." Lecture Topics from Crandall University Religious Studies Program. Accessed April 10, 2013. http://www.abu.nb.ca/courses/NTIntro/Spirit7.htm.

_____. "The Holy Spirit in Pauline Theology." Atlanta Baptist University. March 27, 2006. Accessed April 10, 2013. http://www.freerepublic.com/focus/f-religion/1614888/posts.

Smith, Christian and Patricia Snell. *Souls in Transition: The Religious and Spiritual Lives of Emerging Adults*. New York, NY: Oxford University Press, 2009.

Soelle, Dorothee. *The Silent Cry: Mysticism and Resistance*. Minneapolis, MN: Augsburg Fortress Press, 2001.

Stanley, Charles. *Discovering Your Identity*. Nashville, TN: Thomas Nelson, Inc., 2008.

Tenney, Merril C. *The Zondervan Pictorial Bible.* Grand Rapids, MI: Zondervan Publishing House, 1967.

The Missouri Conference. "College-age Ministries." Accessed October 12, 2012. http://www.moumethodist.org/pages/detail/1521.

Thomas, Frank A. *The Choice: Living Your Passion from the Inside Out.* Chicago, IL: MMGI Books, 2013.

Thomas, Owen C. and Ellen K. Wondra. *Introduction to Theology*. Harrisburg, PA: Morehouse Publishing, 2002.

Thomas, Terry. *Becoming a Fruit-Bearing Disciple.* Raleigh, NC: Voice of Rehoboth Publishing, 2005.

Thompson, Marjorie J. *SOUL FEAST: An Invitation to the Christian Spiritual Life.* Louiville, KY: Westminster John Knox Press, 2005.

Thompson, Phillip E. "Jeremiah 1:1-10." *Interpretation* 62, no. 1:66-68. *ATLASerials, Religion Collection*, EBSCO*host*. Accessed March 19, 2013. http://search.ebscohost.com/login.aspx?direct=true&db=a6h&AN=ATLA0001625982&site=ehost-live.

Thurman, Howard. *The Creative Encounter: An Interpretation of Religion and the Social Witness*. Richmond, IN: Friends United Press, 1972.

Tiffany, Frederick C. and Sharon H. Runge. *Biblical Interpretation: A Roadmap*. Nashville, TN: Abingdon Press, 1996.

Turabian, Kate L. *A Manual for Writers of Term Papers, Theses and Dissertations*, Chicago, IL: University of Chicago Press, 2007.

U.S. Census Bureau. "State and County QuickFacts." Accessed December 11, 2012. http://quickfacts.census.gov/qfd/states/29/2923986.html.

Vickers, Jason. E. *Invocation and Assent: The Making and Remaking of Trinitarian Theology*. Grand Rapids, MI: W. Eerdman's Publishing Company, 2008.

_____. *Minding the Good Ground: A Theology for Church Renewal* Waco, TX: Baylor University Press, 2011.

Vyhmeister, Nancy Jean. *Quality Research Papers for Students of Religion and Theology*. Grand Rapids, MI: Zondervan, 2008.

Wagner, C. Peter. *Your Spiritual Gifts Can Help Your Church Grow*. Ventura, CA: Gospel Light Publications, 2012.

_____. *Finding Your Spiritual Gifts Questionnaire*. Ventura, CA: Regal Books, 1995.

Walsh, Terrance G.S.J. "Writing Anxiety in Teresa's Interior Castle." *Theological Studies* 56, no. 2 (1995): 251-275.

Walvoord, J.F., R. B. Zuck and Dallas Theological Seminary. *The Bible Knowledge Commentary: An Exposition of the Scriptures*. Wheaton, IL: Victor Books, 1985.

Weaver, Cornelius P. *Jesus Goes to College*. Mustang, OK: Tate Publishing and Enterprises, 2011.

Wheaton, John. "A Biblical View of Social Justice." The Christian World View. Last modified November 2, 2008. Accessed December 27, 2012. http://thechristianworldview.com/tcwblog/archives/741.

Willis, John T. "Prophetic Hermeneutics." *Restoration Quarterly* 32, no. 4 (1990):193-207. *ATLASerials, Religion Collection*, EBSCO*host*. Accessed April 28, 2013. http://search.ebscohost.com/login.aspx?direct=true&db=a6h&AN=ATLA0000831895&site=ehost-live.

www.ingramcontent.com/pod-product-compliance
Lightning Source LLC
Chambersburg PA
CBHW080919170426
43201CB00016B/2203